Don't Know Much About

Catholic History

From the Catacombs to the Reformation

Don't Know Much About Catholic History

From the Catacombs to the Reformation

Diane Moczar

Our Sunday Visitor Publishing Division
Our Sunday Visitor, Inc.
Huntington, IN 46750

The Scripture citations used in this work are taken from the *Catholic Edition of the Revised Standard Version of the Bible* (RSV), copyright © 1965 and 1966 by the Division of Christian Education of the National Council of the Churches of Christ in the United States of America. Used by permission. All rights reserved.

Every reasonable effort has been made to determine copyright holders of excerpted materials and to secure permissions as needed. If any copyrighted materials have been inadvertently used in this work without proper credit being given in one form or another, please notify Our Sunday Visitor in writing so that future printings of this work may be corrected accordingly.

Copyright © 2006 by Our Sunday Visitor Publishing Division, Our Sunday Visitor, Inc. Published 2006
11 10 09 08 07 06   1 2 3 4 5 6 7 8 9

All rights reserved. With the exception of short excerpts for critical reviews, no part of this work may be reproduced or transmitted in any form or by any means whatsoever without permission in writing from the publisher. Write:

Our Sunday Visitor Publishing Division
Our Sunday Visitor, Inc.
200 Noll Plaza
Huntington, IN 46750

ISBN-13: 978-1-59276-202-6
ISBN-10: 1-59276-202-6 (Inventory No. T253)
LCCN: 2005933536

Cover design by Troy Lefevra
Interior design by Sherri L. Hoffman

PRINTED IN THE UNITED STATES OF AMERICA

To all my history teachers, living and dead, in San Francisco, Paris, New York, Washington, D.C., and Fairfax, Virginia. They labored valiantly to make a historian of me, and this is their book.

TABLE OF CONTENTS

INTRODUCTION:	What This Book Is and What It Is Not	9
ONE:	The Church in the Roman World	11
TWO:	Catholic Culture: Beginnings	22
THREE:	The Church in the Dark Ages	30
FOUR:	Catholic Thought and Culture in the Dark Ages	40
FIVE:	The Church at the End of the Dark Ages	51
SIX:	Catholic Thought and Culture at the End of the Dark Ages	61
SEVEN:	The Church in the Early Middle Ages	70
EIGHT:	Catholic Thought and Culture in the Early Middle Ages	82
NINE:	The Church in the High Middle Ages: The Twelfth Century	91
TEN:	Catholic Thought and Culture in the Twelfth Century	104
ELEVEN:	The Greatest of Centuries?	115
TWELVE:	Catholic Thought and Culture in the Thirteenth Century	125
THIRTEEN:	The Church in the Late Middle Ages	133
FOURTEEN:	Catholic Thought and Culture in the Late Middle Ages	145
APPENDIX A:	Making Sense of It All	157
APPENDIX B:	Evaluating History Books	163
	Acknowledgments	169
	About the Author	171

INTRODUCTION

What This Book Is and What It Is Not

First of all, this book is not a textbook, with all essential facts about a given period tidily arranged and neatly summarized so you can memorize them for the next test. It is also not a scholarly book with extensive footnotes (in tiny print) for every statement, although it is based on extensive scholarship. Another thing it is not, I hope, is boring.

What it is, then, is a collection of evocative glimpses of the history of the Church, from its emergence in the Roman Empire, through its medieval springtime and high summer, to the bitter autumn that followed those glorious ages. (Further volumes will continue the story.) Each pair of chapters, one on the history of a time period and the second on its culture, will include a few suggestions for further reading, as well as larger questions to think about.

By the end of the book, the reader will have made the acquaintance of a number of interesting characters, both heroes and villains, and have a general idea of how Christian civilization came about, spread, and developed cracks that will become great fissures. In short, he will know something, instead of nothing, about Catholic history.

Such an introduction to a great civilization may be just what many readers are looking for in a book like this. There will be others, however, who will thirst for more. They will wonder: What happened to so-and-so? Exactly when did such-and-such occur? What was the relationship between what was going on in Spain and what was happening in Byzantium at such-and-such a time? Such readers may be students (encountering Catholic history for the first time), teachers, homeschoolers, or amateur historians. The last sections of this little work cannot answer all their questions, but it can point them in the right direction.

Appendix A addresses the issue of "making sense of it all." Here the reader will find hints on organizing historical material so that facts and chronology are clear, with the most significant ones stressed, and so that relationships among the happenings of a given century with what preceded and followed it are made apparent. Appendix B discusses "What next?" Further reading suggestions are what the serious student requires, but lengthy bibliographies — while useful in scholarly books — can be both overwhelming and too rapidly outdated. This section will instead list only a few seminal works on various topics with which the student might begin. It will also, however, give suggestions on how to evaluate the tide of books that are currently being published in every field. How can one avoid getting stuck with a pricey, well-publicized tome that turns out to be either useless for one's purposes or downright lousy history? Appendix B can't prevent that from happening to you, but it can greatly reduce the possibility.

May this book increase your knowledge and understanding of Catholic history, and your love for God, Who is the source of all truth.

CHAPTER ONE

The Church in the Roman World

The world suffers nothing from Christians but hates them because they reject its pleasures.
— St. Justin Martyr

What do you think the following passage describes?

> Once upon a time there was a country. After a revolution in which it overthrew the rule of a foreign king, it became a small republic. Its religion was simple, emphasizing republican virtues such as piety, discipline, patriotism, and simplicity of life; most citizens were small landowners. The people had a talent for practical rather than theoretical accomplishments; they were fine builders, engineers, and administrators.
>
> The country began to expand, at the expense of its neighbors, and conquer native peoples. It developed cities and an urban culture, and began to use slave labor to an increasing degree. It became very wealthy. And as it came into contact with other cultures, it took in ideas and influences from all over the world. People began to say it was losing its own identity.
>
> The early religion declined, and many people took up exotic cults from the East, while intellectuals tended toward atheism. The old republican virtues broke down, and civil war broke out. Birth control, abortion, infanticide, divorce, and homosexuality became common. There was a women's liberation movement.
>
> People stopped reading, except for digests and popular science, and the language became debased. There

was a craze for spectator entertainment: sports of all kinds, but also other spectacles, which grew more obscene and violent as time went on, and the jaded popular taste demanded new thrills.

Pollution was widespread, and many people died of a mysterious new disease. Economic problems, such as inflation and high unemployment, developed. But what many citizens feared most of all was terrorism and war from ruthless barbarian powers to the East.

This is, of course, a word-picture of ancient Rome, from its origins to its decline. But it also bears an eerie resemblance to the history and current state of our own country. Other nations — particularly England — have also viewed Roman history as a mirror of their own world. Certainly it holds many lessons and warnings for those who would understand the growth and decline of civilizations, the overextension of superpowers, and the role of moral decay in political collapse.

THE CHRISTIAN COMMUNITY OF ROME

Readers will recall that St. Peter had become the head of the Church, the first pope, when Our Lord had said those solemn words to him: "You are Peter, and on this rock I will build my church" (Matthew 16:18). When Peter arrived in Rome in the first century, the city thereupon became the seat of the papacy. This did not end with Peter.

St. Peter was succeeded as pope by St. Linus, who is mentioned by St. Paul in his second letter to Timothy; he mentions Linus as one of those sending greetings to Timothy (2 Timothy 2:21). Eusebius says this is the same Linus who became bishop of Rome after St. Peter. St. Irenaeus, writing in the second century, lists twelve bishops of Rome, from Linus to Eleutherius, the latter pope being a contemporary of Irenaeus.

His successors in the papal office became so identified with Rome that an expression was used, "*Roma locuta est, causa finita est*" ("Rome has spoken, the cause is finished"). It was the pope who decided, by virtue of his infallible authority; numerous documents from the end of the first century attest both to the primacy of the pope in the Church and to Rome as the seat of the pope.

THE PERSECUTIONS BEGIN

We pick up the story of the Church during the Roman Empire of the first century: specifically, during the reign of the unbalanced emperor Nero, who was the first to unleash a persecution of the young Christian community. According to the famous account, Nero wanted a scapegoat for the great fire that devastated Rome in the year 64, for which rumor held him responsible. He decided to fix on Christians, who were now being distinguished from the Jews as a separate religion. When Nero held his infamous garden party and, dressed up as a coachman, drove his guests through the gardens, the torches that lit the paths were Christians set on fire. Other party entertainment included watching hunting dogs chase and tear apart Christians sewed into wild animal skins.

In this persecution, which continued for years, both St. Peter and St. Paul, along with many others of the infant community, perished. Not an auspicious beginning for the tiny Church; its triumph over the cruel empire would come, but it was far in the future. Even if we fast-forward one or two centuries, the picture is much the same: in fact, the persecutions, though sporadic, become more systematic and reach throughout the empire. It is true that there were long periods from A.D. 64 to the accession of Constantine in the 300s when Christians were left in uneasy peace. But just consider the cultural milieu in which these Catholics lived. During the Late Roman Empire, while economic and military problems multiplied, entertainment hit an all-time low: watching human beings killing one another or being tortured to death was the pastime of the tens of thousands of spectators who flocked to amphitheaters all over the empire. Theater producers, in an attempt to compete for audiences, provided pornographic activity and even actual murders (using slaves) on stage. Family life went into a catastrophic decline: the authority of the father eroded; birth control, abortion, and infanticide became widespread; and permissive divorce laws led to the constant breakup of homes. Women competed with men in many areas, including outdrinking them at banquets.

Now imagine you are living in the second or third century in Rome and you become a Christian. Your choice will draw you away from almost everything you have taken for granted in your everyday life.

As a Christian, you will practice chastity before marriage and fidelity afterward. You cannot kill your babies, before or after birth, as the Romans routinely do. (As St. Basil will write in the fourth century, "A woman who deliberately destroys a fetus is answerable for murder, and any fine distinction as to the fetus being completely formed or not is not admissible among us Christians.") You cannot indulge in homosexuality. You avoid the circus and the theater, and often the public baths, because of the violence or indecency. You do not read much of the current literature because it is either pornographic or pagan.

There are professions you cannot enter: idol-making, obviously — a big business for the craftsmen of Rome; teaching, because you will have to teach the pagan religion; acting, because it often involves obscene speech and behavior. You cannot even hold most government jobs, because they require ritual worship of the emperor and the gods of Rome.

You stand out like a sore thumb in your social life as well. If you are invited to dinner, you cannot take part in the customary libations poured out in honor of the spirits of the household. You may not send your children to school, for fear they will be imbued with pagan teaching. All of this marginalizes and estranges you from your own society, and can easily arouse resentment and suspicion.

WHY?

Historians still argue over exactly why ordinary harmless Christians aroused such antipathy in both the government and their fellow citizens during the Roman Empire. While many explanations have been given, St. Justin Martyr seems to sum it up best in his *Letter to Diogenes* in the second century.

Justin points out that, while Christians do not differ from their fellow citizens in dress, diet, and such things, their way of life seems strange to their society: "They marry as men do and beget children, but they do not practice abortion. They share tables but not beds. They live in the flesh but not according to the flesh...." Then he compares the Christians in Roman society to the soul dwelling in the body: "The body, though it suffers nothing from the soul, hates it and makes war upon it because it cannot enjoy its pleasures in peace; the world suffers nothing from Christians but hates them because they reject its pleasures."

This is astute psychology. Certainly the neighbors of Christians often denounced them to the authorities out of sheer dislike, as well as more tangible motives of greed for their property, resentment at the loss of customers for idols, and so on. If this happened to you, you stood a good chance of being slowly tortured to death, sometimes over a period of days, as public entertainment.

There has never been, before or since, such a thoroughgoing countercultural movement involving such a likelihood of being tortured to death, and I find it impossible, humanly speaking, to see how it could have got off the ground. Certainly, it is very hard to imagine it taking place today. How many Catholics today would be willing, especially if it meant risking their lives, to dress decently; to avoid indecent movies, magazines, books, and television shows; to practice chastity and firmly reject birth control, abortion, homosexuality, divorce, and professions that endanger their faith (Supreme Court justice?); and to live for heaven rather than for earth? Depressing question. Yet Roman Christians of all classes and ages went cheerfully to horrible deaths, for love of Christ. It amazed the Romans that many of the bravest martyrs were women, even slave women, who might have been expected to be too timid and submissive to face the torturers.

THREE HEROIC MARTYRS

One example of such a brave young woman, martyred in Gaul in A.D. 177, was described in a letter from the local Christian community to fellow Christians in Asia. Some of the pagan slaves of the Christians were arrested and told lies about them to save their own lives, while a few Christians apostatized, which demoralized the rest. Among the Christians interrogated was a slave girl, Blandina, whose arrest worried the rest of the Christians. They feared that she would give way under torture since she was known to be physically weak. Blandina was tortured in so many ways that the torturers finally admitted there was nothing more that they could do to her — yet they got no information out of her except the statements "I am a Christian" and "Nothing vile is done by us." It seems she was brought out for public torture on several different days, each time serving as an example and encouragement to those being martyred with her. By the time she died, even the pagans were forced to admit that they had never seen a woman suffer so much and so bravely.

The martyrdom of St. Perpetua and St. Felicity (or Felicitas) is another example of great heroism on the part of two young women, one a patrician and the other a slave girl, martyred in Carthage in 203. Separated from their families and children (Felicity actually gave birth in prison, but was able to get her baby out to safety), they were unshakeable in their commitment to the Faith and went hand in hand into a nightmare of torture that repelled even some of the spectators. Their whole story is worth reading in detail, and it is fortunately preserved in the diary Perpetua kept of their experiences and that of others suffering with them (see "Reading Suggestions" at the end of this chapter).

In the end, the infant Church survived everything the pagan empire could do to it, even the last and worst persecution unleashed by Diocletian in the early fourth century. While it must have seemed to some, during this empire-wide persecution, that the end of both Church and world was at hand, the reality was that the triumph of the cross was very near: the power struggle that succeeded Diocletian's reign brought to the throne the emperor Constantine, favorably disposed to Christianity because he attributed a crucial victory to the aid of the Christian God. With the Edict of Milan in 313, Christians gained the legal right to practice their religion — this was different from the mere toleration occasionally granted in the past, only to be revoked — and represented a giant step toward the building of a new Christian civilization. Although the Roman Empire would endure into the following century, its days were numbered. Constantine was the last of its great and powerful emperors, and his successors — even Theodosius "the Great" — saw economic, social, political, and military problems spiraling out of their control. In 476, a boy emperor, with the fateful name of Romulus (for the legendary founder of Rome) Augustulus ("little Augustus," for the first and perhaps greatest of the emperors), was deposed by a barbarian chief and the Western Empire met its "official" end, as wave after wave of barbarians flooded into Roman territory.

And what of the Church, as its newfound freedom was once more imperiled by the collapse of the only world Christians had ever known? One might have expected rejoicing on the part of a community that had been so victimized by Rome, but the opposite occurred. "Sobs choke my words," wrote St. Jerome. "Who could believe that Rome, built upon the conquest of the whole world, would fall to the ground?" Other Christian writers were similarly appalled; they simply could not imagine a world not ruled by Rome, not built and ordered and organized by Roman thought and practices. When Constantine had moved the capital of the empire to Constantinople, the headquarters of the Church had remained in Rome.

From the diary of St. Perpetua:

When, she said, we were still under legal surveillance and my father was liked to vex me with his words and continually strove to hurt my faith because of his love: 'Father,' said I, 'do you see (for example) this vessel lying, a pitcher or whatsoever it may be?' And he said, 'I see it.' And I said to him, 'Can it be called by any other name than that which it is?' And he answered, 'No.' 'So can I call myself nought other than that which I am, a Christian.'

"Then my father angry with this word came upon me to tear out my eyes; but he only vexed me, and he departed vanquished, he and the arguments of the devil. Then because I was without my father for a few days I gave thanks unto the Lord; and I was comforted because of his absence. In this same space of a few days we were baptized, and the Spirit declared to me, I must pray for nothing else after that water save only endurance of the flesh. After a few days we were taken into prison, and I was much afraid because I had never known such darkness. O bitter day! There was a great heat because of the press, there was cruel handling of the soldiers. Lastly I was tormented there by care for the child.

"Then Tertius and Pomponius, the blessed deacons who ministered to us, obtained with money that for a few hours we should be taken forth to a better part of the prison and be refreshed. Then all of them going out from the dungeon took their pleasure; I suckled my child that was now faint with hunger. And being careful for him, I spoke to my mother and strengthened my brother and commended my son unto them. I pined because I saw they pined for my sake. Such cares I suffered for many days; and I obtained that the child should abide with me in prison; and straightway I became well and was lightened of my labor and care for the child; and suddenly the prison was made a palace for me, so that I would sooner be there than anywhere else."

Now, while the Eastern Empire survived the barbarian onslaught, Rome had fallen to the barbarians, who would eventually become the Christians of the new age to come — a discouraging prospect in 476, and for a long time thereafter. We will explore that Dark Age, a fascinating time with several important lessons for us, in Chapter Three.

FOOD FOR THOUGHT

The historical sketch given above, brief as it is, raises a number of questions that are worth pondering.

How similar, for instance, is life in the United States today to life in the Late Roman Empire? What are the main resemblances and differences? If American Catholics suddenly faced a persecution like that of Diocletian, how do you think they would react? The possibility may seem remote, but we should remember that until quite recently many Catholics behind the Iron Curtain suffered atrocious tortures for the Faith, and Catholics in China, Sudan, and elsewhere continue to suffer for it today.

READING SUGGESTIONS

This list includes only a few of the many good books that could be recommended for this period. Criteria for the choice of books include readability, historical accuracy, and accessibility. Where a work exists in several editions or reprints, no publisher or date will be given.

General History

The Church of Apostles and Martyrs, by Henri Daniel-Rops (Image Books, 1960). This is an older, very readable work by a major French Catholic historian; it is the first volume of a series on Church history.

The Founding of Christendom, by Warren Carroll (Christendom Publications, 1985). Also the first volume of a Church history series; this volume deals with the origins of Christianity as well as Roman history. Chapters 17 through 20 deal with the period discussed in this chapter.

Church History, by Father John Laux (original 1930 edition reprinted by Tan Books and Publishers, 1989). This is a handy one-volume compendium intended for older high school pupils as well as college students and adults. It is necessarily concise and somewhat outdated, but it includes some primary sources, questions, and reading suggestions.

The Martyrs

There are numerous good collections of saints' lives available, starting with ***Butler's Lives of the Saints***. For information about a specific martyr — such as Blandina, Perpetua, and Felicity — you can't beat the Internet. Websites provide primary documents as well as articles from the early twentieth-century edition of the multivolume *Catholic Encyclopedia* — highly recommended — as well as other good sources. A more recent study of St. Perpetua is ***Perpetua's Passion***, by Joyce E. Salisbury, published by Routledge Press in 1997. This is recommended with reservations. It seeks to place Perpetua in the context of her times and includes valuable information about life and culture in Roman Carthage, the arena and its spectators, and the Christian community; it also includes some trendy (and questionable) assumptions and interpretations. The whole of Perpetua's diary, however, is included in italicized sections within the text.

Novels

Historians often take a jaundiced view of historical fiction because it is so often all fiction and no history, but there are exceptions. For this period of Roman history, there are two classics of both scholarship and literature that are well worth reading. The first is Cardinal Nicholas Wiseman's ***Fabiola*** and the second is Cardinal John Henry Newman's ***Callista***. Of the two, *Callista* is more sophisticated from a literary point of view, including one vividly surrealist passage and a most sinister depiction of sadism. Both authors were classical scholars and bring to life different areas of the Roman world (the city of Rome and Italy in *Fabiola,* North Africa in *Callista.*) Both also use real historical persons as characters. Highly recommended, if you can find them (use the Internet again).

CHAPTER TWO

Catholic Culture: Beginnings

We assert that philosophy, which is characterized by investigation into the form and nature of things, is the truth of which the Lord Himself said, "I am the truth."
— CLEMENT OF ALEXANDRIA

Confronted as it was with hostile paganism at every turn, one might expect that the early Church would have been anxious to separate itself from all Roman influence. In practice, however, this proved impossible. The earliest Christian art, in the catacombs, is in the classical tradition: in some pictures, Christ is portrayed in the manner in which the pagan gods were depicted. Christians writing in Greek and Latin used the forms and vocabulary of their pagan contemporaries. It was almost impossible, in fact, for Roman Christians to imagine a world other than that in which they were living and suffering — Rome had simply *been there* for so many centuries.

Christian education posed a particular dilemma: Where could parents and teachers find uncontaminated textbooks from which children could be taught? As for older students seeking higher education, where was it to be had if not from pagan professors teaching curricula steeped in pagan traditions?

The question became the subject of intense debate, one fraught with the gravest consequences for the future of Western civilization. Could classical culture, pagan as it was, be assimilated by Christianity, or would the Church reject it *in toto* and build a new culture based on Scripture and the writings of the Fathers alone?

A partisan of the latter view was Tertullian. "What has Jerusalem to do with Athens," he asked, "the Church with the Academy, the Christian with the heretic? ... After Jesus Christ we have no need of speculation, after the Gospel no need of research."

There were actually some attempts to teach reading and other basic skills through Christian texts alone, but they were not very successful. It was one thing to remain apart from pagan practices, entertainment, and behavior, and another to escape from all contemporary cultural and intellectual influences.

THE CULTURAL DEBATE

Tertullian's contemporary, Clement of Alexandria, took the opposite view. He argued persuasively that since God is the source of all truth wherever found, the many truths found in Greek philosophy and the other arts and sciences of the past were not to be rejected. The Christian should form his intellect on the logic, mathematics, arts, and philosophy of his predecessors in order to be better equipped to receive and defend the truths of the Faith; secular learning could be a preparation for the higher truths of Revelation.

Fortunately, it was Clement's view that prevailed in the Christian community, thus preparing the way for the great synthesis of classical learning and Christianity that would create the future civilization of Europe. At times, it seemed a close call which way the debate would go; had the Tertullian faction won, the whole heritage of ancient culture would have been in danger of vanishing from the world, with no one caring to preserve it or copy the manuscripts that contained it.

The result for education was that, except in a few cases, Christians did not establish their own schools in the Roman world, even where they were not being persecuted. They utilized secular schools, but added an intense instruction in Christian doctrine, by parents to children, by the Church to catechumens, and by the clergy to the whole community through liturgical readings, preaching, and Christian literature.

In his *Education in Antiquity*, the great historian Henri Marrou quotes St. John Chrysostom's advice to parents on teaching their children. Parents, he says, should tell their children Bible stories, such as the accounts of Cain and Abel, and Jacob and Esau, in an interesting and systematic way.

> When the child really knows the story, wait a few days and then one evening say to him, "Tell me the story of the two brothers." And if he begins to tell you about Cain and Abel, stop him and say, "No, I don't mean that one, I mean the one about the other two brothers, the ones whose father gave a blessing." Then remind him of a few important little details, without mentioning the brothers' names. When he has told you the whole story properly, go on to the next part...."

The early Christian family, then, was deeply involved in the religious training of children, while making use of the Roman school system; it was only after several centuries that the time for truly Christian schools would be ripe.

BEGINNINGS OF CATHOLIC LITERATURE

The Roman period was very rich in great Christian literature in both Latin and Greek, and St. Jerome, St. Augustine, St. Ambrose, and numerous other scholars produced the very first works of Christian theology, philosophy, exegesis, and history. We often fail to realize what a monumental task these thinkers had, especially in creating the new discipline of Christian theology.

To cite just one formidable problem, there was simply no vocabulary in Greek or Latin for much of what Christian writers wanted to say. Theological terminology had to be created, either by introducing new words or giving new meanings to existing words. There was no Latin word for "person," for instance, yet the concept of the person is an essential one for Christianity. The Latin word *persona* generally referred to the mask used by actors to identify a character in a play. Christians therefore gave *persona* a new meaning to express what we now mean by a human or angelic person; by the early sixth century, St. Boethius used it as meaning "an individual substance of a rational nature" — a definition that fits both angels and men.

It should be noted that the Greek philosopher who most influenced Christian writers was not the down-to-earth, realist, scientific Aristotle, but Plato the idealist.

(Idealism here does not mean noble ideals, but a basic view of reality: for Plato, material things are reflections or imperfect copies of their perfect forms that exist somewhere in "the world of ideas." The "forms" are a higher reality than what we experience with our senses. Plato's idealism is also revealed in his political treatise, *The Republic,* in which he portrays a perfect state — a utopia — rather than political systems as they are.)

Platonism appealed to Christian thinkers partly because of its "other worldly" character — the world of ideas was an escape from the depraved and sordid society of the Roman Empire. For Plato also, unlike for Aristotle, the study of nature seems to have held no attraction; this attitude, too, would have consequences for later Christian thought. The forms, though, could be understood as ideas in the mind of God; thus Platonism could be made to seem compatible with Christianity, and its influence lasted for many centuries.

THE FATHERS AND DOCTORS OF THE CHURCH

The writings of the Fathers and Doctors of the Church are so numerous and varied that there is no space even to begin a discussion of them here. For the reader interested in sampling them, a good place to start might be one of the numerous editions of St. Augustine's autobiography, or a collection of letters of the Latin Fathers, especially those of the often-irascible St. Jerome. Such works provide a more revealing glimpse into the personalities of the Fathers than do some of their learned treatises. The sermons of the Fathers also make fine reading, and are available in many editions.

It is worth mentioning here two of the most influential Christian women of the period (apart from the martyrs). St. Augustine's autobiography provides us with an unforgettable portrait of his mother, St. Monica, who is a model for all mothers of wayward children. Similarly, the mother of Emperor Constantine, St. Helena, suffered much from the actions — murder included — of her son. She also, at an advanced age, accomplished the tremendous feat of identifying many of the sacred sites in the Holy Land and saving them from destruction. The value of that achievement is incalculable, but there is much more to St. Helena's story, which can be found in biographies of her. (Start with *Butler's Lives of the Saints* or the old *Catholic Encyclopedia* entry, available online; just do a Google search for "St. Helena.")

There is no room here, either, for a discussion of the several major heresies that loomed so large in Roman Christian polemics and involved pioneering decisions and definitions by the earliest Church councils and popes. One of the heresies, Arianism, will be addressed in a subsequent chapter because of its historical impact on events in northern Europe.

There is another aspect of early Christian life, however, that deserves mention: the impulse that led so many men and women to flee the corruption of their surroundings and take up a radically different way of life in the desert. This impulse amounted almost to a mass movement of disheartened urban Christians; even major intellectuals and writers, normally based in the cities of the empire, often went into seclusion in remote places for at least part of their lives. One thinks of St. Jerome heading for the cave in Bethlehem (taking his library with him, however) and complaining that the memories of the dancing girls of Rome followed him even there.

The corruption of imagination and memory caused by the constant bombarding of the senses with moral depravity is surely something to which we can relate. With us, however, it does not seem to have given rise to any countercultural mass movement away from the sick stimuli that daily prick us. The Christians of the Roman Empire reacted differently. In their thousands they sought an austere life in the desert, either as hermits or organized into loose communities, striving to purify themselves and come to union with God in undistracted prayer and labor. St. Anthony (or Antony), whose life

---

Here are two of the many incidents artlessly recorded by the monastic writers.

- A group of monks, sober and recollected, were out for a walk on a desert path. A group of nuns happened to be coming the opposite way on the same path, so the monks courteously stepped off the path to let them pass. As the mother superior swept by she remarked, "Humph. If you were real monks you would not even have noticed that we were women!" (Sometimes men can't do anything right.)

- There was a hermit on a mountaintop who felt sure he had made great progress and come very close to God, so he asked the Lord if this were so. The Lord said, in effect, "Well, you're pretty good, but so-and-so and so-and-so are much further along than you are." Disappointed and perhaps somewhat piqued, the monk beetled down from his mountain and went in search of the paragons of virtue he had been told about. What astonishment was his when he located them and found that they were housewives! They told him they had married two brothers and lived their lives of work and prayer simply, and in the love of God. The hermit was much humbled by this experience.

Fortunately, a gifted historian, Helen Waddell, has produced an extremely readable translation of many of these documents in *The Desert Fathers* (first published in 1936 but reprinted by Vintage Books in 1998). Here is a really attractive work, both entertaining and suitable for spiritual reading, that illuminates a whole world of thought and life that would otherwise seem impossibly remote. The book abounds in similar stories, some funny, some touching, all full of the flavor and vitality of early Christian life.

was written by his friend St. Athanasius, was the first to found such monasteries and write a rule for them, as St. Benedict would do some centuries later for a different type of monastic community.

There is a special character of charm, simplicity, and humanity — as well as austerity — to the desert way of life, and it has been preserved in extensive collections of Latin and Greek texts.

It is surely a mark of the supernatural origin of the Church that it not only survived centuries of bloody persecution, ostracism, and torture within the Roman Empire, but that it produced throughout that same period great writers, scholars, monks, and saintly men and women from every walk of life, most of whom (the orthodox Catholics, that is) were extraordinarily articulate and clear-thinking. Their intellectual gifts were partly due to the culture and education of Rome and Greece, but even more to the dynamic inspiration of the Holy Spirit, stimulating their genius to produce writings and works that have endured throughout the ages.

In the breakdown to come, when Rome could no longer even hold itself together administratively, it would be those same educated Christians, many of them saints, who would step into the breach — such as Pope St. Gregory the Great, who organized garbage collection in Rome while writing his voluminous moral and theological treatises. But that is another story.

FOOD FOR THOUGHT

Would the educational methods of the early Christians work for Catholics today? Do most American Catholic parents spend time teaching their children Bible stories, as St. John Chrysostom advised? How much religious education, or continuing education, do most Catholic children and adults actually receive these days?

What about the early Christian impulse to flee the corruption of contemporary society? Does anyone do this now, or have the contemplative religious orders largely disappeared? Could it be that Catholics are so saturated with secularism that they no longer see why they should try to escape it?

READING SUGGESTIONS

In addition to the works mentioned above, there were numerous biographies of the saints, especially of the martyrs, written from the earliest Christian period. Many of these have not been translated, or are otherwise inaccessible to the general reader. I am including here more-recent works on two saints, one from the third century and one from the fourth, drawn from original Roman accounts.

Life of Saint Cecilia: Virgin and Martyr, by Dom Prosper Guéranger. This is a reprint of an English translation, but it seems to be the only book I own that indicates neither date nor publisher, nor place of publication. It appears to be a shorter version of Guéranger's massive French study of the saint and the society of her time, but who translated it and when are a mystery. In any case, the author has drawn extensively on Roman sources, including conversations reported by her biographers and other details that provide a vivid portrait of the young saint. (Some modern historians have questioned the historical value of some of these sources, but there is also much to be said for their authenticity. We need not go into that vexed question here.)

St. Martin of Tours, by Henri Ghéon (Sheed and Ward, 1946). This is a translation of a charming little book by a major Catholic writer and dramatist about a little-known fourth-century saint. The author mentions several primary sources that he seems to have utilized extensively, though he is concerned more with the drama of Martin's life than with documenting its details. Like all of Ghéon's studies of saints, it makes for fine reading.

CHAPTER THREE

The Church in the Dark Ages

The vices of our bad lives have alone conquered us.
— SALVIAN

The "fall" of Rome, much debated by historians, was not one catastrophic event. Although the last of the Roman emperors had been deposed and a barbarian chief had taken his place in 476, not everything changed all at once. Indeed, had the only change been one of rule, Rome might have continued as it had for centuries; after all, non-Italians had worn the purple before, and Rome had had trouble with the uncivilized tribes on the borders of the vast empire for many generations.

What was different in the late fifth century, besides the worsening of the economic situation, was the seemingly endless masses of barbarians suddenly overwhelming the borders from the north and east. Called variously "Germanic" or "Gothic" peoples, they were tribes with distinctive characteristics who had — for the most part — fled into the empire in sheer panic. They were, in fact, pushed.

THE HUNS

The pushers were an extraordinary people from north of China called the Huns. Following a failure to defeat China in the early 400s, the whole people, apparently, riding swift Mongolian ponies and traveling with their tents and gear, began to march six thousand miles west. The tribes they encountered on the Eurasian steppes fled in panic before them, forcing tribes further west to move, which they did — into the Roman Empire.

Neither Germans nor Romans had seen the like of the Huns before, with their fierce tactics, rapid movements, Mongolian

The Church in the Dark Ages

features, and unpleasant odor. They camped in what is now Hungary (part of the Roman province of Pannonia) and seemed for a time to settle down. Some Huns even served in the Roman army. All this changed when a man of genius and ruthless ambition came to the throne of the Huns: his name was Attila, and he had plans for a great Asiatic empire to replace the Roman; quite possibly, he hoped to conquer the whole known world.

There is no space here to detail the fascinating personality of Attila, a man of many contradictions. But we can get some idea of it from the fact that he was skilled both at manipulating people through diplomacy and at the deliberate use of terror and atrocities; he said he "would show force in order not to have to use it," and he liked to call himself "the most detestable man in the world." When the pope called him "the Scourge of God," Attila seemed well pleased.

John Carey, in his collection of texts called *Eyewitness to History* (Harvard University Press, 1987), gives us a glimpse of a dinner with Attila through the eyes of Priscus, an ambassador of the Eastern emperor. He describes the dining room, its furnishings, the order in which the guests were seated, and how — although the guests were served lavish food in gold and silver dishes — Attila ate sparingly from a wooden plate. He was also dressed very simply. Two of his sons (he seems to have had dozens) were also present: "The eldest son was sitting on Attila's own couch, right on the very edge, with his eyes fixed on the ground in fear of his father."

Priscus then recounts the series of toasts, one for each guest, and the multicultural entertainment befitting the polyglot diners.

> After the songs a Scythian entered, a crazy fellow who told a lot of strange and completely false stories, not a word of truth in them, which made everyone laugh. Following him came the Moor, Zerkon, totally disorganized in appearance, clothes, voice and words. By mixing up the languages of the Italians with those of the Huns and Goths, he fascinated everyone and made them break

out into uncontrollable laughter; all, that is, except Attila. He remained impassive, without any change of expression, and neither by word or gesture did he seem to share in the merriment except that when his youngest son, Ernas, came in and stood by him, he drew the boy towards him and looked at him with gentle eyes. I was surprised that he paid no attention to his other sons, and only had time for this one. But the barbarian at my side, who understood Italian and what I had said about the boy, warned me not to speak up, and said that the seers had told Attila that his family would be banished but would be restored by this son.

Poor first-born son, of such a father.

RESISTANCE OF THE WEST

Once they opened hostilities, the lightning campaigns of the Huns in both the Eastern and Western parts of the empire devastated and terrified the population. They wiped out the merchant settlements on the Danube, destroyed seventy cities and fortresses in the Balkans, and forced even Constantinople to make terms. Then they turned to western Europe, striking city after city. At Paris, St. Genevieve took charge of the defense when the men wanted to flee, and elsewhere Christian bishops led the resistance.

Just when all seemed lost, a Roman general, Aetius, was able to piece together an alliance between what was left of the Roman legions and the Visigoths he had just defeated before the Huns came. In the Battle of Chalons, in 451, the combined forces were able to stand firm against the Hunnish advance. The morning following the battle revealed that the Huns had disappeared, to the relief of the spent army. What had happened, however, is that Attila was now headed for Rome. Down the Italian peninsula rode the Huns, spreading destruction and scattering the people (some to islands in the Adriatic, which then became the city of Venice).

Roman pagans, still powerful in the 450s, had been loudly complaining that it was the existence of Christianity that had called down the wrath of their gods and brought the barbarians, but here came their answer. As Attila approached Rome, a procession of men dressed in white, chanting, came out to meet him. At their head was Pope St. Leo I, come to talk to the Scourge of God. No one knows exactly what was said, but when the pope returned to the city he told the emperor, "God has saved us from a great peril."

The Huns left as swiftly as they had come, probably with a sizable ransom, but also because Attila was so impressed with spiritual authority (he had shown this in earlier incidents). Soon after arriving back in Hungary, Attila died in a sort of spectacular fit, and the Huns quickly vanished to the east, never to return.

THE IMPORTANCE OF THE EVENT

This whole episode proved two things: first, that the pagan gods had been unable to save Rome and the Christian God had done so, and second, that Romans and barbarians could actually cooperate in meeting a common threat, as they had done at the Battle of Chalons. This cooperation of Romans, barbarians, and the Church would be the foundation for a new civilization — which, unfortunately, was still centuries in the future.

Meanwhile, overwhelming problems remained. The Germanic tribes were mostly hostile to Rome and the Church

> During the Vandal siege of Hippo, in North Africa, St. Augustine addressed the people: "Enough of your weeping and wailing! Are you not yourselves responsible for this fate which is overwhelming you? 'These are difficult and dreadful times,' people are saying. But these times are part of us, are they not? The times are what we have made them! Yes, we are all guilty, but we have been promised mercy."

because they had been evangelized by Arian missionaries, following the condemnation of Arianism at the Council of Nicaea in 325. They differed widely in character: some simply settled down, like the ones who took over Switzerland, and later started making cuckoo clocks and chocolates. Some, particularly the Vandals, cut paths of devastation for hundreds and even thousands of miles as they rampaged through the empire, killing and destroying. They crossed into North Africa and were at the gates of St. Augustine's city as he lay dying.

THE VOCATION OF THE FRANKS

Of all the peoples who now took possession of chunks of the former Western Empire, one would be of major significance for the future of civilization and Christianity in western Europe: the Franks. Unlike most of the tribes, they had not adopted Arianism but remained pagan; they were at least not heretics, but they had obscure grudges against the Romans from earlier dealings with them. That changed when a Catholic Burgundian princess, Clotilda, married a Frankish chief named Clovis in the late 400s.

St. Clotilda was one of a considerable number of Christian women of the period who willingly married barbarian leaders, with the hope of converting and civilizing them. In the case of Clotilda and Clovis, the hope was fulfilled in an extraordinary way. They seem to have been a devoted couple; and although Clovis remained pagan, he allowed their children to be raised Catholic out of love for his wife. His willingness to accede to her wishes was sorely tested when their first child died soon after receiving Baptism. So this was how "Clotilda's God" repaid His followers! Such was his love for Clotilda, however, that he consented to have their next child baptized. To his horror, this child also became ill after receiving Baptism, but fortunately recovered.

Clovis must have given thought to Clotilda's religion long before the famous event with which his conversion is associated. In 496, just twenty years after the deposition of the last emperor, Romulus Augustulus, in Rome, Clovis was engaged in a battle against another tribe, and the Franks were getting the worst of it. Clovis finally declared he would pray to Clotilda's God for victory, and against heavy odds victory was granted to him. He then took instructions in the Catholic Faith from St. Remigius, the great apostle to the Franks, and was baptized at Reims.

During the ceremony, there occurred a miracle that seems well attested by at least one trustworthy eyewitness. St. Remigius was at the point where the baptismal ceremony required the use of holy chrism, but the assistant bearing the oil was unable to get through the enormous crowd in the cathedral. St. Remigius was seen to look up to heaven in prayer, and suddenly a dove descended bearing a vial of oil to the bishop. The dove then disappeared, and the saint anointed the king of the Franks with the mysterious oil. This vial of miraculous oil would be used in the consecrations of the French kings until it was destroyed by the French revolutionaries (a piece of it, with a little of the oil, was later recovered and used for the last time in the consecration of Charles X in the early nineteenth century).

Thus began the alliance of the Kingdom of the Franks with the Church that would be at the heart of the Catholic civilization of the West, as France became the "eldest daughter of the Church" and the champion of Catholicism against Arianism. The capital of the Salian Franks was to be Paris. As long as Clovis remained a pagan, St. Genevieve (such was her authority over the Parisians) refused to allow him to enter the city. As soon as he was baptized, she opened the gates, and was thereafter a great friend of Clotilda and adviser to the royal couple.

THE STATE OF EUROPE IN THE DARK AGES

There was, in hindsight, much to look forward to in the sixth, seventh, and eighth centuries, but unfortunately for those who lived through them they were anything but promising. Even where the barbarians did not destroy buildings, art, water systems, and books, they had no notion of how to maintain them. For a while, clergy and other educated men were able to keep some urban institutions and systems running, but it was a losing battle; by the year 1000, there were fewer than twelve towns left on the whole continent of Europe (all with fewer than ten thousand inhabitants), and no cities at all — and this on the ruins of an urbanized empire with population centers housing hundreds of thousands of people. Rome, from a maximum population of a million or more in its heyday, dwindled to a village of dwellers among the ruins, with those once magnificent buildings slowly reduced to stone quarries by residents building defensive walls.

The descendents of Clovis fragmented the unity he had achieved in the Frankish realm, with the rulers of the fragments fighting one another as well as other tribes. They fell into such degeneracy and incompetence that they were called the "Do-Nothing Kings," and the business of ruling was delegated to an official called the "Mayor of the Palace." We shall see what will come of this.

What about the hopes of those Late Romans who "prayed God to send them the barbarians"? Did the uncivilized at least bring an influx of new blood and new energy to the old empire? Sadly, as historian Henri Daniel-Rops remarks, "barbarians and civilized exchanged vices." True, masses of former pagans were adopting Christianity, but the ignorance and low moral level of the new converts were such that, especially with a corresponding decline in the numbers of educated clergy, the result was often the lowering of religious and moral standards throughout society.

Even before the fall of Rome, not all converts could be called wholehearted Christians. In the fifth century, Pope St. Leo was horrified when he saw worshipers about to enter St. Peter's first making a ritual sign in honor of the sun, a feature of the pagan religion of Mithra. Now, the imperfectly converted were joined by the barely converted, and it is no wonder the moral and spiritual level of Dark Age society was very, very low. Clerical celibacy became rare in some areas. Even the monasteries, which had spread over much of the Western Empire and preserved in varying degrees the wise Rule of St. Benedict, were infected with the general ignorance and moral decay; their recruits, after all, were children of their melancholy age. To make matters worse, the local landowners were asserting control over both the lands and the administration of the monasteries — going so far as to appoint abbots, usually from their own families, to achieve their goal (the infamous practice of "lay investiture").

There were some bright spots, of course, not the least of which is the miracle of Ireland. While Europe was sunk in tribal strife and cultural decline, Ireland was in its golden age. It had never been conquered by the Romans, and was spared — for a long time — barbarian conquest. When the legions were withdrawn from England, as imperial rule crumbled and not even the great Arthur (Artorius, "the Restitutor") could hold off the Saxon invasions, Ireland was not affected. Following the missions of, first, Palladius and then Patrick, in the 400s, Ireland experienced conversion to Christianity, the flourishing of Christian culture, and a proliferation of monasteries that were remarkable for their learning and the purity of their way of life.

The "Isle of Saints and Scholars" was sending missionaries to the continent by the century following its conversion, perhaps earlier. In 590, St. Columban (or Colombanus) was rebuilding a monastery in Gaul that had been destroyed by the Huns, and creating centers of holiness among the decadent Merovingian descendents of Clovis as well as in Italy — and he was only one of a multitude of Irish monks who kept the Faith alive when it seemed to be sinking in a sea of barbarism and decadence.

By the 600s, things seemed to be settling down in some places, as tribes consolidated their power and at least stayed put. Economic conditions were still grim. The great Eastern emperor, Justinian, had failed in his attempt to reunite the Roman Empire, leaving the West even more isolated from the civilized (and organized) East as the Byzantines withdrew from nearly all their bases in Italy. Still, one could hope that things would eventually look up. Could they get much worse?

They could. In 632, a man named Mohammed died in Arabia and his followers burst forth from their homeland in a spectacular tidal wave of conquest. Islam was on the march. This new creed that was founded on a few basic principles, such as one God and simple religious rituals, had galvanized the Arabs and made them a new nation, committed to spreading their religion by conquest. They believed in conquering the world for their God, and subjecting those who would not convert to death (if they were pagan) or inferior status in Muslim society (if they were Christians or Jews). We will pick up the story of the Christian West at this point in Chapter Five.

FOOD FOR THOUGHT

Are there any comparisons to be made between the world of the Dark Ages and that of the early twenty-first century? Migration is an important historical theme: Can we make any comparisons between the influx of various groups of immigrants into the modern West and the migrations that overwhelmed the Western Empire? There are obviously important differences; are there any similarities? How about the state of the Church then and now?

READING SUGGESTIONS

General History

The Church in the Dark Ages, by Henri Daniel-Rops (1959 edition republished by Phoenix Press, 2001). This is a readable account of the period, especially Chapter 4 on the conversion of the barbarians and Chapter 5, "Christians of the Twilight: Sinking into the Night of Barbarism."

The Building of Christendom, by Warren Carroll (Christendom College Press, 1987). The first seven chapters of this work deal with the Dark Ages.

The End of the Ancient World and the Beginnings of the Middle Ages, by Ferdinand Lot. This is a scholarly work by a fine French historian, first published in English in 1931 and revised in 1951.

The Gateway to the Middle Ages: Italy, by Eleanor Shipley Duckett (1938 edition republished by University of Michigan Press, 1988). Anything by Duckett is worth reading, in my opinion. Her profound scholarship is cloaked in a style that makes her books read like novels. This one deals with Italy in the sixth century.

The Gateway to the Middle Ages: France and Britain, by Eleanor Shipley Duckett (1938 edition republished by University of Michigan Press, 1988). This is the shortest of Duckett's *Gateway* books, but the first section — which takes up most of the volume — succeeds in providing a vivid picture of life in France at this period, including details about Clovis, Clotilda, and others drawn from some fascinating primary sources. The account of Britain in the same period is necessarily brief, given the lack of reliable contemporary sources dealing with the Saxon conquest. As usual, however, the author sheds light on both the age and its more interesting characters.

The Gateway to the Middle Ages: Monasticism, by Eleanor Shipley Duckett (1938 edition republished by University of Michigan Press, 1988). Roman monasticism, Celtic monasticism, St. Benedict, and St. Gregory the Great are included in this work. The author brings Benedict and Gregory to life with sympathy and fine writing.

There are many other books dealing with this period, some more specialized, such as Geoffrey Ashe's ***The Discovery of King Arthur*** (Henry Holt and Company, 1987). For those who want to believe in Camelot, there is encouragement in several recent works, of which this is one.

CHAPTER FOUR

Catholic Thought and Culture in the Dark Ages

... the plunging / Of the nations in the night.
— G. K. CHESTERTON

The end of the world was long ago, / And all we dwell to-day / As children of some second birth, / Like a strange people left on earth / After a judgment day.... / When Caesar's sun fell out of the sky / And whoso hearkened right / Could only hear the plunging / Of the nations in the night."

This famous line from Chesterton's *Ballad of the White Horse* reflects the disorientation and pessimism of many during the Dark Ages, when the only "world" they had known was fallen, and the night of barbarian turbulence went on and on. Gradually, literacy declined with the disappearance of schools. A few generations after 476, we find a text by a man who takes pains to tell us that he was taught by a tutor employed by his parents, and that the tutor was in turn taught by a private instructor, who had received instruction from a still earlier scholar.

Learning was becoming a private treasure, passed down by individual teachers to a few pupils. Already before the fall of Rome, the Latin language was becoming debased; slang, sloppy style, and "digests" of books (to suit readers with short attention spans) were common. In the mouths and infrequent pens of the barbarians, the Latin of Cicero disappeared and a simpler and less elegant tongue took its place. The future Medieval Latin would become, later, a flexible and eloquent vehicle for poetic, philosophical, and scientific expression. During the darkest centuries, however, Late Latin must have sounded to the educated few as painful as the Late English conversations of some of my students sound to me. Historian Henri Daniel-Rops calls the period "one of the most painful that Christianity has ever known, even up to modern times.... Only the Church, guided by a transcendent ambition, pursued her course unwaveringly, and in working to her own supernatural ends she became the most effective means of ensuring the salvation of civilization."

CULTURAL DARKNESS

The great danger, of course, was that, given the lack of trained minds and precise language, the Faith itself would not be adequately transmitted to future generations. Books were still preserved in the monasteries, and the invaluable work of making copies of them still went on. The monastic scribes, however, were less and less able to comprehend what they were copying, and errors crept into their texts. (Had they been able to understand their texts, they would have been horrified at some of the scurrilous Roman material they reproduced, on the somewhat naive premise that all books were precious.)

One day the great learning locked in the monastery libraries would teach a new generation of scholars, but in the Dark Ages there were few to understand what they contained. We have correspondence from a couple of Dark Age readers who had come upon a mathematics text and were puzzling over what a right-angled triangle might be. Still, learning did survive, and we got through the darkness, as Kenneth Clark puts it in his *Civilisation*, "by the skin of our teeth."

SMALL SURVIVALS

Learning, like purity of morals — which suffered a drastic decline — and of Church teaching, survived in pockets. We will look briefly at some of the pockets, and consider a few of the often-unsung heroes of an unheroic age.

Ireland, discussed in the previous chapter, was one such pocket, producing educated missionaries who went out into Dark Age Europe and beyond, lighting candles of belief and literacy as they went. Elsewhere, as in Britain, the barbarian raids had destroyed Christian institutions and culture, so the work of conversion had to be done again. The daunting enterprise of rebuilding a literate Christian culture in Britain began with the arrival of St. Augustine of Canterbury in the late 500s, while Irish missionaries to Britain worked at the same task. In Gaul, following the death of Clovis, religion, culture, and political organization all declined precipitously, and the struggle to hold on to the purity of the Faith, and to remnants of literacy and education, was grim. As for Italy itself, seat of the papacy, the situation was brighter in the earlier part of the Dark Ages, but depressingly worse by the 700s.

ITALY

To begin with Italy, we can first note the situation under the Ostrogothic king, Theodoric, who had defeated an earlier Gothic ruler to assume the throne at the end of the fifth century. He was in some ways a good ruler, who relied on edu-

---

The elegant Greek-speaking Arius, a priest of third-century Alexandria, was the founder of what became a long-lasting heresy; in fact, it is still around in various forms. His main idea was that Christ is not God; He is something more than a mere man, but still a created being. Arius embedded this notion in such elaborate and polished rhetoric that he took in many simple Catholics, among them many bishops.

Condemned at the Council of Nicaea, the followers of Arius migrated to the northern barbarian tribes and spread a sort of hybrid Arianism — suitable for uncivilized and superstitious warriors — among them. As a member of one of those tribes, Theodoric was an Arian.

cated Romans like Cassiodorus and St. Boethius to assist him. He also kept up the buildings and roads. But he had a bad temper that could have tragic consequences. Although Theodoric was an Arian, his relations with the papacy in the beginning of his reign were cordial.

Theodoric was angered, however, by the attempts of the Eastern emperors (who were then still Catholic) to oppose Arianism and promote Catholicism. At one point, he abruptly ordered Pope John I to go to Constantinople as his emissary; when the pope returned, Theodoric received him angrily (we do not know exactly why) and threw him into prison. Pope John died soon after, and is venerated as a martyr. The king was also responsible for the death of the great Boethius, his former associate, and that of Symmachus, friend and father-in-law of Boethius, who dared to grieve for him. The king seems to have been overwhelmed with remorse following these atrocities, but that hardly helped his victims.

ST. BOETHIUS

While in prison, St. Boethius wrote the masterpiece for which he is best known, *The Consolation of Philosophy*.

Philosopher that he was, Boethius imagines a dialogue with Lady Philosophy to consider what comfort the intellect may draw from examining a great variety of issues such as what reason can know of God, how futile is the pursuit of worldly goods, and why God permits evil. Translated into many tongues, even during the Dark Ages, quoted and analyzed by scholars from the early Middle Ages to the present (including St. Thomas Aquinas), it is one of the great books of the West.

Boethius contributed much more to the Catholic civilization of the future, however. He wanted to translate the works of Aristotle from Greek into Latin. Although some of his works were lost, his translations of the logical treatises as well as extended quotes from Aristotle in some of his other works ensured the survival of at least some knowledge of Aristotle in

> St. Boethius begins *The Consolation of Philosophy* by bemoaning his fate, alone in his prison cell. "Why, O my friends, did ye so often puff me up, telling me that I was fortunate? For he that is fallen low did never firmly stand."
>
> He then imagines Lady Philosophy appearing and sending away the "Muses of poetry" that have instigated his laments: "Who has suffered these seducing mummers to approach this sick man? Never do they support those in sorrow by any healing remedies, but rather do ever foster the sorrow by poisonous sweets. These are they who stifle the fruit-bearing harvest of reason with the barren briars of the passions: they free not the minds of men from disease, but accustom them thereto."
>
> She then commences an extended conversation with him to bring him "the consolation of philosophy."

the West. This was a tremendous contribution to learning, since it would be several centuries until the entire Aristotelian corpus would be recovered.

The loss of such a vast body of work is a little hard to understand. Part of the explanation may be the lack of interest in Aristotle's vigorous realism and scientific work in the later Roman Empire, when Neo-Platonism was so much in vogue. Another possibility is that many of the manuscripts perished in the fire that consumed the vast library of Alexandria, Egypt, in Hellenistic times. Barbarian destruction would account for the loss of still more copies. Even what we have today is mostly the course notes of Aristotle's students, and we know only the names of several treatises that remain lost to us.

Boethius had a reputation for learning in many fields, even in his twenties. We find Theodoric asking him to send a water clock to the Burgundian king who had asked for one; apparently Boethius was known for understanding the workings of such things. Similarly, when Clovis, king of the Franks, wanted a harp player, it was up to Boethius to find one because of his knowledge of music. He wrote theological treatises, notably on the Trinity; in a treatise against the heresies of Eutyches and Nestorius he came up with the classic definition of the term "person," and the formulation of the doctrine of one person and two natures in Christ. He also supported the training of the mind through the seven liberal arts, as a preparation for philosophy, and wrote treatises on the four higher arts: arithmetic, music, geometry, and astronomy. Here again, he exercised a great influence on the development of education in the Middle Ages and beyond.

Boethius was the great transmitter of classical science, philosophy, and the arts from his own era to the other side of the Dark Ages; Daniel-Rops also calls him the last Roman writer and the last "lay" writer, since most of the great literary figures of the future would be monks.

POPE ST. GREGORY THE GREAT

After Theodoric's death in 526, wars between the Eastern Empire and the Goths devastated Italy; a brief restoration of imperial rule was cut short by yet another barbarian invasion, that of the Lombards. These latecomers included a miscellany of other barbarians in their large army; they fell upon Italy while it was in the grip of a plague, conquered most of it, and ruled for two hundred years.

It would be tempting to study papal history during this period, but it is far too big a subject and includes too many complex issues (such as the controversy over Pope Honorius I) to fit into an essay on Dark Age Catholic thought. The outstanding pope of this period was Pope St. Gregory I, the Great, who reigned from 590 to 604, during the Lombard hegemony in Italy. It was a time of plague, floods, and violence, described thus by Gregory:

> Sights and sounds of war meet us on every side. The cities are destroyed; the military stations broken up; the land devastated; the earth depopulated.

Gregory's job was overwhelming. He had to maintain Roman independence from Lombard control, and do it largely by bribing the barbarians with money raised from papal estates. He had to feed the population and perform most of the work of a civil administration that no longer functioned. He had to maintain delicate relations with the Eastern Empire, and at the same time deal with the reconversion of barbarian Europe (it was he who sent St. Augustine to England.)

Besides all this, Gregory's written output was voluminous: over eight hundred letters, as well as many treatises on all sorts of subjects. They are not the elegant philosophical treatises of Boethius, nor, perhaps, is the Latin style as pure as his. Gregory lacked the time for elegance, and circumstances influenced the kind of things he wrote: those hundreds of letters — to emperors, barbarian kings, missionaries, and clergy — dealt with practical as well as spiritual affairs.

Gregory's celebrated *Pastoral Care* seems to have been originally his own meditations on the high office he had reluctantly assumed; but as a treatise on the selection, life, duties, and practical qualities of good clerics, it became enormously popular. Father John Laux writes in his *Church History*, "No better book on the life and duties of the clergy has ever been written. If he had written no other work than this, St. Gregory would deserve to be ranked amongst the Fathers and Doctors of the Church."

Gregory may not have invented "Gregorian" chant, but his musical reforms and other contributions greatly enriched Church music and promoted the training of musicians. Looking at his own writings in the light of what he called the "deep and clear torrents of the blessed Fathers Ambrose and Augustine," Gregory saw his work as "a mean little trickle." That trickle, however, as Eric John's biographical compendium, *The Popes*, puts it, "could satisfy the thirsts of simpler minds better than could the 'torrents of Ambrose and Augustine.' They had still breathed the air of a civilization now vanished from Western Europe; Gregory belonged to the new, medieval world, and men had a sense of being at home with him."

ST. BEDE OF ENGLAND

We return to England, the reconversion of which was so dear to the heart of Gregory. Here the figure of major importance is one particularly dear to the hearts of historians: St. Bede the Venerable — "and we may add the still beloved," as Henry Osborn Taylor writes in *The Mediaeval Mind*. According to Daniel-Rops, Christopher Dawson said that Bede represents the highest point reached by intellectual culture in the West during the period between the fall of the Western Empire and the ninth century. (I could not find this statement in any of the Dawson works I consulted, but it is hardly an exaggeration.)

St. Bede was born on the estates of the monastery of Sts. Peter and Paul at Jarrow, in northeast England. He was taken by relatives at the age of seven to live in the monastery, and remained there for the rest of his life. He apparently never traveled, as so many of his contemporaries did, paying repeat visits to Rome and Gaul. He was never a bishop or even an abbot. What he loved was learning and teaching, and he became perhaps the greatest Dark Age transmitter of sacred and secular learning to later ages: "I have always held it my joy to learn, to teach, and to write."

Bede's studies were wide-ranging, and the manuscript collection of his monastery was amazingly rich. He was interested in science, nature, geography, grammar, and above all in Scripture and the writings of the Fathers and Doctors of the Church. He even knew some Greek, which was extraordinary at a time when the knowledge of Greek in the West had virtually disappeared.

The goal of Bede's large literary output was to pass on to his students and other readers the treasures he found in the precious books that were not available to them. His scriptural commentaries give evidence of his keen analytical skills in detecting copyists' errors, discussing the precise meaning of words, the chronological order in which we must see events that are often related differently in Scripture, and the various levels of meaning found in scriptural passages.

It was not until four years before his death at sixty-two that St. Bede wrote the book for which he is best known today: *History of the Church of the English People*. He had earlier written the lives of the abbots of his monastery and others, and possibly historical sketches, but this is a landmark work, beginning with the invasion of Julius Caesar in 55 B.C. and ending in 731 — a time when England was experiencing violent upheaval after decades of general peace. Historian Eleanor Shipley Duckett writes, "It is our gain that he lived to write of the widening life of the Church in England at a time when the teachings of Mahomet and hordes of the Saracens were threatening the Church across the seas. And since he wrote with a scholarship and passion for accurate knowledge to which Gregory [of Tours] could not pretend, he is still to us the 'Father of English History.'"

On the day of his death, Bede was still dictating his translation of the Gospel of St. John into Anglo-Saxon, but he was not quite finished. The boy taking dictation reminded him that there was still one chapter left, but that it would be hard for the saint, in his state of health, to answer more questions about it.

"No, it is easy," said Bede. "Put your pen in the ink and write fast."

Later on, the boy told him there was one sentence left.

"Good! Write it!" said Bede.

"Now all is written."

"It is well, you have spoken the truth," said Bede, "for 'it is finished.'"

Supported by his young scribe, Bede chanted the *Gloria* and died as it came to an end. One of the brightest lights in the Dark Ages had gone out.

There is a lesson here on how easily true religion and learning can be lost. Even though they may survive in books, their transmission to individual minds and hearts requires teachers steeped in doctrine and scholarship, and those teachers in turn must have achieved a high level of formation. It has been one or two generations now since — with a few exceptions — we have seen that level of competence in theology, classical languages, and the liberal arts. For all our technological and scientific knowledge, we live in a dark age of fuzzy faith and semi-learning. Like the Late Romans, lapsing little by little, and quite unconsciously, into sloppy speaking, imprecise thinking, immorality, and finally barbarism, we may not realize how dark our age is until the darkness lifts and we can look back on it.

Is this an exaggeration? As long as I'm exaggerating, I might as well go further out on a limb and recommend an unusual (some would say bizarre) novel about life in a future Dark Age in which the central figures are monks who have somehow preserved Latin and the Faith following a nuclear cataclysm. The book is *A Canticle for Leibowitz*, by Walter M. Miller Jr., originally published in 1959. While it is a page-turner, it also stimulates thought on the earlier Dark Age, on our present age, and what things would (will?) be like after its collapse.

FOOD FOR THOUGHT

The reader may find so many contemporary parallels here that it is almost superfluous to suggest them. Part of the fascination of history is that it looks different to every generation; its color changes, as it were. In civilized times the Dark Ages might seem remote — like a bad memory nearly erased by the march of civilization.

Today, the period has a strange attraction for many thoughtful people. The prospect of a nuclear disaster wiping out what we know of civilization is not unthinkable; when Roman civilization died, learning survived in the monasteries.

Where would it survive today? And what of the state of learning in our modern universities?

To anyone who has taught college for any length of time, the increasingly rapid decline in student quality — in intellectual ability, diligence, and honesty, as well as in level of academic preparation — is alarming. If students are to graduate, courses must be "dumbed down," requirements modified, and assignments made as cheat-proof as possible, because students cannot be trusted.

Is this how civilization is slowly lost, or is it just that we are coming into a new kind of technological civilization?

READING SUGGESTIONS

Most of the works dealing with this period are specialized studies, some of the best of them in languages other than English. Here are three that serious readers might enjoy.

The Mediaeval Mind (vol. 1), by Henry Osborn Taylor (London, 1911). This is an older and partially outdated work by an apparently non-Catholic historian. I love it because of its readability and because Taylor has that gift of sympathy for his subjects that makes them live for the reader.

Anglo-Saxon Saints and Scholars, by Eleanor Shipley Duckett (Macmillan, 1947). This is yet another fine study of Dark Age personalities, this time in England. Her word portraits of St. Bede and three of his compatriots read like engaging stories, though based on meticulous scholarship.

The Love of Learning and the Desire for God, by Jean Leclercq, O.S.B., (Fordham University Press, 1961, 1982). This translation (from the French) is a series of lectures given to young monks in Rome in 1955-56, of which some deal with Dark Age topics.

CHAPTER FIVE

The Church at the End of the Dark Ages

Fight those who believe not in Allah nor the Last Day, nor hold that forbidden which hath been forbidden by Allah and his Messenger....

— Koran 9:29

Catholics in the eighth century may be forgiven for not thinking they were nearing the end of the Dark Ages. If anything, life was looking darker and the news was all bad. Hordes of barbarians, unified by a new religion that preached jihad against the "infidel," had been pouring out of Arabia and devastating North Africa; the ancient African Church had nearly disappeared from history. The Mediterranean had become a Muslim lake, perilous for dwellers along its shores, while even inland areas in Italy and elsewhere were plundered by fierce raiding parties. Constantinople, the capital of the Byzantine Empire, itself had been attacked.

Even worse, Arabs and their Berber allies had swept into Spain and conquered the whole peninsula — conquered it, that is, except for one tiny spot in the Asturias Mountains. There, King Pelayo held out with a small band even though his advisers, including a bishop, advised him to surrender. Pelayo refused, saying that the hope of the Visigothic people was in Christ, Who would deliver them: "This little mountain will be the salvation of Spain...." So it would prove to be, though much later in history; the seed of Spain's resistance to Islam would grow relentlessly over the centuries to become the triumphant *Reconquista*.

The chief of the besieging army, on the other hand, felt he had wasted enough time. "What are thirty barbarians perched on a rock?" he sneered. "They will inevitably die." And he proceeded to the next step of his program to take over Europe, by invading France. It was there, however, that the hope of Catholics would be rekindled and the tide of darkness would, most improbably, begin to turn.

THE BATTLE OF TOURS

When the Moors (as the Arab/Berber invaders were termed) swarmed into France, they were not met by a worthy descendent of Clovis. There were kings in Paris, of course, but they had long been negligible factors in national life. For generations, the decadent and incompetent kings had turned over the tedious work of governing to the Mayors of the Palace, and it was one of these, Pepin, who had united the realm in the decades preceding the Moorish invasion. It was Pepin's son, Charles, called "the Hammer" (Martel), who scraped together a Frankish army to meet the Moors as they rode north.

The clash would be one of the turning points of European history. Scholars argue whether the Moors were in a position to conquer Europe at the time, or whether they simply intended a raiding foray to test the waters for future reference. In any case, they received a decisive answer to any questions they might have had about the strength of the Franks.

The battle has been variously called the Battle of Tours and the Battle of Poitiers, though in fact it took place in an area between the two towns. The Moorish horses had long, sharp spikes on their breastplates for the purpose of impaling unhorsed opponents, and the struggle was long and grim. In the end, the Franks were victorious, and the tide of Islam flowed back to Spain — at least on land.

Perhaps it was a wake-up call for the "do nothing" Merovingian kings, polishing their tiddlywinks game in the safety of the royal palace. The prestige of Charles Martel passed to his son, Mayor of the Palace Pepin the Short.

(Reader: "How short?" Author: "Little bitty guy, exact dimensions unknown.") It was during the reign of Charles that St. Boniface left England for the German mission lands, but it was Pepin who invited him to reform the whole western Frankish Church; the indefatigable Boniface had spectacular success among the German tribes, and everywhere he promoted the authority of the papacy and the need for Catholic rulers to defend it.

It was also Pepin, a strong and competent ruler in spite of his stature, who wrote to the pope and posed the question of who should have the royal title in a nation: he who had inherited it or he who was actually performing the job? Pope St. Zacharius replied, "It is better that he who possesses power be called king than he who has none." Thus the royal authority should be held by the one who actually exercised it; whereupon the Franks escorted the last Merovingian into a monastery — possibly to his secret relief — and Pepin was crowned king.

A NEW ROYAL FAMILY

Pepin is notable for the concept of kingship he expressed: "To us the Lord hath entrusted the care of government." This is not the old tribal kingship idea, with the state merely the personal possession of the king, but the foundation of Catholic legitimacy: the rule of a king chosen by God and answerable to Him for the temporal and spiritual well-being of his subjects. It was Pepin, too, who established the Papal States, providing the popes with a much-needed buffer zone around Rome as protection against the marauding Lombards and other barbarian raiders.

More could be said about Pepin, but it has been his fate to be overshadowed in history by his great son Charles: Charles the Great, in fact, or Charlemagne, who succeeded to the throne of the Franks in 768. With him, a new era opened for the peoples of Europe, as well as for the Church. This period of economic, political, and cultural progress is called "Carolingian," so closely is it identified with the person of Charles himself.

CHARLEMAGNE

Unlike his father, Charles was oversized (they ran to extremes in that family), more than six feet tall, of imposing appearance, with reddish hair and beard — the whole picture marred only by his squeaky little voice (perhaps inherited from little Pepin?).

Charlemagne's first concern was to establish order throughout the sprawling realm of the Franks, and to defend the borders against enemies — by treaties, if possible; by war, if necessary. In thirty years he waged something like sixty campaigns, half of them in person. They ranged from fighting the Muslims in Spain and the Basques in the Pyrenees (the historical setting for *The Song of Roland*), to attacking the wild Avars in what is now Hungary, to pacifying northern Italy.

Charlemagne's biggest headache was the pagan Saxon tribes, who broke promise after promise not to renew attacks on the Franks until, all else having failed, Charlemagne forced Christianity on them. He resettled them within his empire — which by this time included the heartland of Europe, minus Spain, and they settled down and ceased to be a threat. Of course forced conversion was never sanctioned by the Church, since acceptance of Christianity must be a free act. In this case, however, even Catholic writers consider that in the case of the Saxons Charlemagne really had little choice.

A true turning point in European history occurred on Christmas Day in the year 800, when Pope St. Leo III, who had been restored to his throne by Charlemagne, following kidnapping and ill treatment of the pontiff by some of his many enemies, made a fateful decision. The Frankish ruler entered St. Peter's for midnight Mass a king, and left it an emperor: crowned Roman emperor by the pope and acclaimed by the congregation. Despite the still-controversial questions of whether Charlemagne was pleased or angry about the papal action and exactly what was in the mind of the pope, the coronation of Charlemagne represents two important developments.

First, the "restoration" of the Western Roman Empire, so many centuries after its disintegration, was a milestone in the history of the West, and of that Europe which the great king already largely controlled. The dream of European unity under a Catholic ruler would survive the empire's demise (the modern European Union, with its anti-Catholic laws and principles, is a sort of obscene caricature of it). As for Byzantium, the throne of the Eastern emperors was technically vacant at the time (it was held by a woman) — and though later rulers huffed and puffed over the outrage to their imperial dignity, one finally gave in and began to address Charlemagne as "my imperial brother."

The second reason for the significance of the coronation lies in the shift in the geographical focus of Western civilization that it represents. Almost from time immemorial, the Mediterranean had been the center of European history: *Mare Nostrum*, the Romans called it, "Our Sea." It was the ancient waterway by which armies, commerce, culture, ideas, and missionaries traveled among three continents. Now it had fallen into enemy hands, and the economic, political, cultural, and religious life of Europe must develop elsewhere — in the northwest, in fact. Hence the famous statement of historian Henri Pirenne that, "Had there been no Mohammed, there would have been no Charlemagne." (This is something of an exaggeration, but not by much.) The popes had been increasingly turning their attention to the north all through the Dark Ages, both to promote the spread of the Church in northern Europe and to seek the protection of the newly powerful Catholic kings against such enemies as the Muslims and the Lombards. The ancient alliance of the papacy with the Franks, which had begun with Clovis, was now bearing fruit.

In economic affairs, Charlemagne promoted numerous reforms that were desperately needed in those depressed times, and the agricultural innovations that began under him would later produce a true agricultural revolution. He also issued standardized coins to facilitate local trade. Foreign trade was a more difficult problem. The Muslim conquests had greatly disrupted European contacts with the East, but Charlemagne was able to achieve a modest increase in long-distance trade by using Jewish merchants who could move in both the Muslim and Christian worlds. (His own foreign contacts included, as a sort of royal pen pal, the legendary caliph of Baghdad, Harun al-Rashid, who sent him a baby elephant as a gift.)

THE CAROLINGIAN RENAISSANCE

Charlemagne also put all his resources behind a great campaign of education and cultural revival, known as the Carolingian Renaissance (discussed in the following chapter on the culture of the late Dark Ages). It is no wonder that soon after his death the emperor was being honored as St. Charlemagne, with a feast celebrated on January 28 in his capital of Aachen, and also in France, though he was never included in the Roman calendar; St. Joan of Arc invoked him along with St. Louis IX.

Objections have been raised as to his morals, since one of his biographers refers to "concubines" he supposedly had after the death of his last wife. Dom Prosper Guéranger, historian and author of *The Liturgical Year*, defends very vigorously the holiness of Charlemagne's life in the account he gives in the January 28th entry in volume two of the Christmas volumes of *The Liturgical Year.* He insists that the term "concubines" refers to wives who were not recognized as queens, and that Charles married them successively. His opinion seems based on solid sources, and his analysis of the motives of Charlemagne's detractors is persuasive. Modern historians like Henri Daniel-Rops and Eleanor Shipley Duckett take a different view of the character of the great emperor, also using primary sources; but Guéranger's arguments appear hard to refute. Perhaps Charles the Great deserves at least the benefit of the doubt.

CHAOS IN ROME

During the period following Charlemagne's death in 814, his empire was divided into what would become France and Germany, with an ill-conceived Middle Kingdom in between that would be fought over by its neighbors until the mid-twentieth century. As the ninth century wore on and the tenth began, so did the third wave of barbarian invasions to batter Europe since the fall of Rome. The second, Muslim, wave continued, with Rome itself threatened in the mid-ninth century, while two new groups of barbarians mounted formidable attacks on the West.

The papacy, too, with a few shining exceptions, reached what may be considered its all-time low point — though I can

---

As a bishop, Formosus had been in charge of a mission to Bulgaria and been accused of trying to obtain the office of Bulgarian patriarch. His condemnation was temporary, but according to the canon law in force at the time it seems to have cast doubt on the validity of his election as pope in 891. (Documentation is lacking for much of this confused period.) He certainly was involved in the political intrigues of Roman factions, though he himself was said to live a holy life.

Pope Formosus became embroiled in the struggles of various claimants to remnants of Charlemagne's empire, and at one point was imprisoned by his enemies while an anti-pope was set up. By the time he was released, he was a very old man near death, which occurred in 896.

The following year his corpse was disinterred by members of one of the warring factions, dressed in his former pontifical robes (complete with the hair shirt he used to wear), and charged with violations of canon law. Pope Stephen VII pronounced the deceased guilty and annulled all his acts, including ordinations — thereby invalidating his own episcopal consecration! The corpse was stripped, mutilated, and dragged through the streets of Rome. Finally buried, it was again dug up and thrown into the Tiber River. Pope (if he was pope) Stephen the VII (or VI) ended up strangled. Historian Warren Carroll's comment on this incident is terse but apt: "Hell hates Rome."

think of one or two other periods that might qualify for this dubious distinction. Papal elections were often manipulated by powerful factions; popes were deposed and replaced at frequent intervals (some reigns lasting only months or even days); and the gruesome affair of the disinterment, "trial," and profanation of the corpse of Pope Formosus occurred.

VIKINGS AND MAGYARS

The decline of royal political control allowed the feudal lords in northwestern Europe to gobble up Church lands with impunity. Meanwhile, pagan Viking raiders began to stream out of Scandinavia and devastate the coasts and waterways of Europe, while from the East masses of Magyar horsemen swept out of Asia to raid the West repeatedly until they were decisively defeated in the mid-tenth century. There are incidents of people fleeing the coastal areas to escape the Vikings, only to fall victim to the Magyars (called Hungarians by Europeans, because they were erroneously thought to be a later generation of Attila's people).

Still, the age was not as dark as it had been. There were isolated bright spots, such as the reign of Alfred the Great in England, king of Wessex, hero of G. K. Chesterton's *The Ballad of the White Horse*, who is famous for more than providing his people with exemplary government, promoting learning, and translating Latin works into Anglo-Saxon (discussed in the next chapter). Had he not been successful in his lengthy guerrilla warfare against the Danes, finally repulsing their formidable raids, we would have lost both his literary output and perhaps the rest of Anglo-Saxon culture. "And there was death on the Emperor / And night upon the Pope; / And Alfred, hiding in deep grass, / Hardened his heart with hope," as Chesterton puts it in *The Ballad of the White Horse*.

No matter how dark things became in the mid-tenth century — the "age of lead" — Charlemagne's empire *had* existed; the Carolingian Renaissance *had* occurred; and the memory of those achievements kept the period from being as black as the time of the first wave of barbarian invasion. It needed only the cessation of the most recent raids, a thorough reform of the Church, and the restoration of political authority to produce a new and glorious Catholic civilization. A tall order, certainly; yet it was to happen, as we shall see.

FOOD FOR THOUGHT

What is the greatest danger for a country or a civilization: external invasion, internal quarrels, or moral and political corruption? We have seen examples of all of these coming together in the Late Roman Empire, and we see them again — though to a lesser degree — at the end of the Dark Ages.

What do you think should have been the first priority of the leaders of the post-Carolingian world? Are there any resemblances at all between that time and ours, or were the late Dark Ages one of those periods that have no modern parallel?

READING SUGGESTIONS

Alfred Duggan's *The Right Line of Cerdic* (Pyramid, 1967) is a fictional treatment of the life of Alfred the Great by a well-known Catholic novelist of the first half of the twentieth century.

Alfred the Great: The King and His England, by Eleanor Shipley Duckett (University of Chicago Press, 1958), is a short, readable account of the king's life and achievements, with emphasis on his contributions to learning.

St. Dunstan of Canterbury: A Study of Monastic Reform in the Tenth Century, also by Eleanor Shipley Duckett (W. W. Norton, 1955), is another fine portrait of an important figure of this period. Since St. Dunstan was born in the early tenth century, a few years after the death of Alfred, a consecutive reading of their biographies provides a view of England throughout most of the Dark Ages.

A useful little work that combines information with selections from primary texts is ***The Era of Charlemagne***, by Stewart C. Easton and Helene Wieruszowski (Van Nostrand, 1961), while Christopher Dawson's ***The Making of Europe*** (Sheed and Ward, 1932; Catholic University of America Press, 2002) is a classic treatment, by a major Catholic writer, of the history of Christendom from the Late Roman Empire through the ninth century.

CHAPTER SIX

Catholic Thought and Culture at the End of the Dark Ages

He most zealously cultivated the liberal arts, held those who taught them in great esteem, and conferred great honors upon them.
— EINHARD, IN HIS BIOGRAPHY OF CHARLEMAGNE

As we have seen, the center of Catholic civilization in the West had largely shifted from the Mediterranean world to northern Europe during the Dark Ages, particularly to the realm of the Franks. In that region, the great cultural development of the eighth and early ninth centuries was surely the Carolingian Renaissance.

Toward the end of Merovingian rule in the kingdom of the Franks, learning had nearly disappeared. That it did so only "nearly" and not "entirely" was due to the work of the Irish missionaries in restoring monastic discipline, ascetic ideals (even among some of the laity), and literacy in Frankish territory. Still, not only was ignorance widespread but writing itself — meaning a standard legible script, one of the treasures bequeathed by the Romans to their empire — had greatly deteriorated. (I don't care to draw a modern parallel, because it will remind me of the dozens of illegible final exams I correct every semester.)

THE CAROLINGIAN RENAISSANCE

When he came to the throne of the Franks, Charlemagne put all his resources and prestige behind a campaign of education. Even under the Merovingians, efforts had been made to prepare the sons of noblemen for administrative posts and to ensure a minimally literate clergy. But Charlemagne's love of education went far beyond these immediate practical goals. As Pierre Riché puts it in his *Daily Life in the World of Charlemagne*:

> On the day of their anointment, Carolingian kings were entrusted with the mission of leading their people to salvation. They had to be given the means of knowing the Truth and renouncing pagan beliefs and superstitions. It was a great ambition. Artisans, merchants, and the rural masses were to be instructed in the Christian religion while pagan populations in newly conquered regions were to be evangelized. Charles sought to imitate Josiah who, "preaching, correcting, exhorting, struggled to bring the realm which God entrusted to him to His true worship." The king desired that the men and women of all his lands should be instructed in the Christian message. For that, he needed well-trained clerks.

Indeed, the need was great, and probably most critical among the clergy. Knowledge of Latin had so declined among them that we hear of an eighth-century cleric who baptized "*in nomine patria et filia*" ("in the name of the nation and the daughter"). A letter of Charlemagne describes mail he received from monasteries in which, he writes,

> We have recognized in most of these letters both correct thoughts and uncouth expressions; because what pious devotion dictated faithfully to the mind, the tongue, uneducated on account of the neglect of study, was not able to express in the letter without error.... We began to fear lest perchance, as the skill in writing was less, so also the wisdom for understanding the Holy Scriptures might be much less than it rightly ought to be. And we know well that, although errors of speech are dangerous, far more dangerous are errors of the understanding.

EDUCATION AND SCHOLARSHIP

The old palace school at Aachen, Charlemagne's capital, now opened its door to promising students of all classes and ages. It seems girls were also taught there, and there is evidence that this was also true in the countryside. A contemporary poem refers to Charlemagne's young daughter, Gisela, "who studies the stars in the stillness of the night." (Charlemagne himself was especially interested in astronomy; in fact, he was so interested in many subjects that he often sat in the classroom with the other students to learn, and sometimes taught after he had learned.)

Perhaps Charlemagne appreciated learning all the more because there were so many gaps in his own education. He had learned to read, and he could speak a number of languages, but the skill of writing eluded him. According to his biographer Einhard, Charlemagne would keep a tablet under his pillow and practice writing at night when he could not sleep: "However, as he did not begin his efforts in due season, but late in life, they met with ill success."

Numerous contemporary documents testify to the scope of the teaching throughout the empire, during the reigns of both Charlemagne and his successors. Mention is made of the often ingenious methods employed, and the humane treatment of very young students, with due provision made for playtime and exercise. (Modern educational propaganda to the contrary, John Dewey and the educational progressivists were not the first to think children should be kindly dealt with, as Roman, Dark Age, and medieval texts prove.)

Where was Charlemagne to find teachers? He first recruited a learned English deacon, Alcuin, who was on his way home from Rome when he met, and impressed, Charlemagne. Alcuin was already fifty, an advanced age in those days, but after thinking it over he accepted the post of head of the palace school and developed it according to Charlemagne's vision. The rest of the faculty was assembled from all over Europe, wherever real scholars could be found. The dedicated little group, and their students and *their* students, formed a tiny intellectual elite that would carry learning through the last storms of the Dark Age winter and into the springtime of the Middle Ages.

While hardly household names to us, men like Alcuin, Einhard, Lupus of Ferrières, Walafrid Strabo, and the great Hincmar (archbishop of Reims) laid the foundations for the great flowering of medieval culture; without them, it would hardly have been possible. It was they who unlocked the secrets of learning that had been preserved only in the ancient books copied in the monasteries, often by monks who could not understand them; they therefore stressed the mastery of Latin, the need for books, and the great care required for the copying of texts. Their original work deserves mention also, but this is not the place for such a discussion.

It is pleasant to think of the little group of professors and students gathered in the palace school, with Charlemagne in their midst, calling one another by Latin nicknames, asking one another Latin riddles, and above all exploring through conversation all those new realms of thought that had been opened up to them through their studies and their books. Alcuin himself, while much beloved — like St. Bede — as a teacher, did not make original contributions to the literature of his time, as did some other members of the little Aachen circle. But in his second (or third) career, Alcuin did something almost as important.

When Alcuin was sixty-five, he retired from the headmastership of the palace school (in some ways a proto-university) and became abbot of the monastery of St. Martin of Tours. He continued his busy correspondence on political affairs and other affairs, answering the many questions he received from students and colleagues on theological and other matters. He also became a zealous librarian, building up the monastery's book collection, acquiring rare manuscripts from England and elsewhere, and promoting the accurate copying of the precious texts.

BOOK PRODUCTION AND A NEW STYLE OF WRITING

This production of books was thus a major contribution of the Carolingian Renaissance. Kenneth Clark, in *Civilisation*, reminds us that "people don't always realise that only three or four antique manuscripts of the Latin authors are still in existence: our whole knowledge of ancient literature is due to the collecting and copying that began under Charlemagne, and almost any classical text that survived until the eighth century has survived till today."

Even in the sixth century, under the Ostrogoths in Italy, Cassiodorus had insisted in a treatise written for his monks on the great importance of the work of the scribe, especially in copying the Scriptures: "Every word of the Lord written by the scribe is a wound inflicted on Satan. And so, though seated in one spot, with the dissemination of his work he travels through different provinces... people hear the means by which they may turn themselves away from base desire and serve the Lord with heart undefiled." Later on he cautions, "But lest in performing this great service copyists introduce faulty words with letters changed or lest an untutored corrector fail to know how to correct mistakes, let them read the works of ancient authors on orthography.... I have collected as many of the works as possible with eager curiosity.... [If you] read [them] with unremitting zeal, they will completely free you from the fog of ignorance...."

Alcuin's zeal for his monastic library was echoed throughout the Carolingian world. In some monastery or other, perhaps in a few simultaneously, a new script was developed that Clark describes as "the most beautiful lettering ever invented": the Carolingian minuscule. It is only by comparing pictures of Roman inscriptions and the almost illegible Merovingian script with the new style that one can appreciate how advanced it was, and why it is called the ancestor of our own writing and printing. Letters are clearly formed, with capitals and small letters distinguished, and words are separated by spaces. This sounds commonplace, until one tries to read a Roman inscription all in capitals, with no separation between words, or the scrawling chicken scratch that both preceded and followed the Carolingian period. (The Italian Renaissance revived the Carolingian minuscule after it had fallen into disuse, and passed it on to us.) It was also during the time of Charlemagne that manuscripts began to be beautifully illustrated with pictures of all types; this was an innovation because early illuminations had generally been purely abstract designs.

Latin was the indispensable language of learning, indeed of civilization itself. But Charlemagne recognized, like Alfred the Great, that many ordinary people could not follow Latin sermons. He therefore ordered that "each priest should have a collection of homilies containing all the necessary admonitions for the instruction of our subjects in the Catholic faith.... And each should see to it to have these homilies openly translated into the rustic Romance or German language so that all the people may well understand their content."

This mention of the vernacular languages reminds us that Charlemagne's realm included people of many ethnic and linguistic groups, some speaking tongues related to Latin — such as the future Italian, French, and Spanish languages — and others various Germanic dialects. According to Einhard, Charlemagne was very interested in the great poems and stories of the Germans and had some of them written down, though they have not survived: "He ... caused the unwritten laws of all the nations under his rule to be tabulated and reduced to writing. He also wrote out and committed to memory the rude and very ancient songs which told of the exploits and wars of the kings of old. He also began a grammar of the speech of his country.... He likewise gave the proper names to the twelve winds, for previously names were known for hardly four...." He may also have encouraged the vernacular tongue in the part of the empire that would become France, for we have a treaty from the time of Charlemagne's grandsons that includes the language that would become French.

ALFRED THE GREAT

The story behind Charlemagne's transcriptions of oral vernacular literature and his encouragement of translations recalls the work of King Alfred the Great in England.

Either personally or through his strong encouragement of the work of others, Alfred saw to it that classics of the previous centuries were translated into Anglo-Saxon, starting with Pope St. Gregory the Great's *Dialogues* and then his famous *Pastoral Care*. The king personally translated for his people works on the Church, geography, and other subjects in a simple and popular style, sometimes adding simple material of his own composition.

> In a letter from the late ninth century, after the Danish raids had been afflicting the land, Alfred the Great compares the current situation of Anglo-Saxon culture with its earlier glories:
>
> "I have called to mind, too, how eager in those days religious orders were for teaching and for learning ... and how men from abroad came to seek wisdom and knowledge in this land; and how we now have to get such men from without, if we are to have them at all. So utterly has knowledge fallen away in England that when I began to rule there were very few men on this side of the Humber who could understand their [Latin] Mass-books and Office in English, or even translate a letter from Latin into English...."
>
> He also refers to the Danish devastations:
>
> "On all this I thought, and I thought also how, before all was destroyed and burned, I saw the churches throughout England standing full of treasures and books. We had then a great multitude of servants of God; but very few of them knew what was in their books. Not one whit could they understand of these books, because the books were not written in their own native speech...."

ART AND ARCHITECTURE

Before we leave this period, something should be said of Carolingian art, though mere words are insufficient. However, here is one example.

When Charlemagne was on his way back to Aachen after his coronation in Rome in 800, he stopped at Ravenna and much admired the great Byzantine church with its splendid mosaics. When he got home, he began to build a palace chapel modeled after it, including the first mosaics ever used in a German church, and pillars he had somehow got from Ravenna. His Frankish architect was incapable of producing an exact replica, but what he did achieve was an imposing and beautiful building that still stands.

Charlemagne had numerous other building projects, many of them palaces, but since they were made of wood they perished in the barbarian waves that swept over his empire later in the ninth century. It was a beginning, though; a great sign of what was to come in the north of Europe once the sun came out again.

FOOD FOR THOUGHT

What entitles someone to be called "the Great?" Consider the qualities of Pope St. Gregory the Great and Charlemagne: Are any of them common to both men? Can you think of any figures in modern history that deserve the title of "Great?" If Charlemagne were to return to his former realm today, what main differences — apart from technological change — would he notice? Consider factors such as the Latin language, which facilitated international communication in his day. What has taken its place? What do you think he would find most distressing and why?

READING SUGGESTIONS

The books mentioned in Chapter Five are also relevant here, as are some of the works on the Dark Ages mentioned in earlier chapters. Two works by Eleanor Shipley Duckett, one already referred to in the previous chapter, are highly recommended: ***Alfred the Great: The King and His England*** (University of Chicago Press, 1958) and ***Carolingian Portraits — A Study in the Ninth Century*** (University of Michigan Press, 1962). My one criticism of the latter book is that the impression given in her brief introductory sketch of Charlemagne is the very opposite of the one we find in Dom Prosper Guéranger's *The Liturgical Year*; one would think they are describing two different people. Most of her book, however, deals with major figures of the Carolingian Renaissance such as Einhard.

For anyone interested in medieval literature, a standard older work, ***The Dark Ages***, by W. P. Ker (Hyperion Press, 1955), is worth reading, or at least consulting. The author was one of the great authorities on the literature of the period, and the sections in this book on the contributions of Alfred and the Carolingian scholars, as well as many authors whom I have not mentioned, are illuminating.

CHAPTER SEVEN

The Church in the Early Middle Ages

A morning dawned radiant on the world.
— THIETMAR OF MERSEBURG,
ON THE YEAR 1000 IN HIS *CHRONICLE*

"One might have said," wrote a chronicler, "that the whole world was shaking off the robes of age and pulling on a white mantle of churches." He was referring to the time about the year 1000, when a new spirit seemed to blow over Christendom, and the churches that were being built everywhere were no longer poor wooden things, destined for destruction by the next wave of barbarians, but pure white stone that gleamed in the sunlight: it was in many ways the early springtime of Christendom. Some would argue that spring had already come during the glorious reign of Charlemagne, or under the Ottonian emperors in the tenth century. There was lots of winter mixed in with those springs, however.

By the year 1000, (though Henri Daniel-Rops puts it later, around 1050) winter was largely over. The invasions had ceased, except for the raids of the converted but still warlike Normans; badly needed reforms had begun in the Church; nations were being organized under competent Christian kings; and the standard of living was on the rise.

Popular writers used to claim that a general hysteria had gripped Europe before the year 1000; a sort of pre-Y2K foreboding, combined with premonitions that the Millennium was up and the Last Judgment at hand. There had certainly been enough upheavals and low spots in the tenth century to justify late Dark Age pessimists, but historians now know that there never was a general expectation of the end of the world in A.D. 1000. For one thing, calendars differed from place to place. A merchant from Germany might travel to a trade fair in southern France and find some of the locals putting their affairs in order because "Doomsday" — New Year's Day, 1000 — was next week. "Nonsense," he would chuckle. "We started 1000 six months ago and nothing happened then, did it?"

So word got around that not only was calendar reform needed, but that things might actually be getting better instead of worse. Gradually a new energy — one might say spring fever — spread throughout the West.

RENEWAL

It is hard to know where to start with the list of Things That Got Better. Perhaps it is best to start at the bottom, with agriculture.

Beginning with the time of Charlemagne, a number of improvements had begun to take hold in the way land was farmed in Europe; taken together, they constitute a true agricultural revolution that is one of the turning points of European economic history. The rediscovery of Roman farm technology, such as the waterwheel, was a step forward, as was the development of the heavy plow, the horseshoe, and the new horse harness. The dense forests that covered much of western Europe were being cleared for farming, and on the coast dikes would soon be created to hold back the sea and enclose fertile soil. Perhaps the most productive innovation was the creation of the three-field system of crop rotation, which produced an increase in agricultural output, which then could support a larger population. Soon, as Europe moved beyond subsistence farming, not all hands were needed for food production and increasing numbers of people began to take up trades and crafts — not just on the feudal estates where they lived, but in villages that were increasing in number and size.

THE FEUDAL SYSTEM

A word about feudalism. Its complex roots go back to Roman times, but we don't want to make that trip right now. Germanic customs also influenced its development. Suffice it to say that the system was essentially a coping mechanism that emerged during the chaos following the breakup of the Carolingian Empire.

Only a powerful local warlord could maintain order and public safety in the areas under his control, and he could only do it if he was supported by other fighting men loyal to him: his vassals. The emergence of cavalry as the main type of fighting force during the Dark Ages meant that warriors needed both horses and large plots of land on which to graze them. The lord therefore would often give his vassals, in return for their loyalty and if he could manage it, pieces of land of which they in turn became the lords. Thus the "feudal pyramid" was constructed: the most powerful lord was at the top, with a sizable chunk of land and his vassals under him; these vassals, in turn, had their neighboring chunks of land and their own vassals, again with their own estates. When danger threatened (or a tempting prospect for a nice little war turned up), the lord could summon his vassals, who in turn summoned their own vassals, and a feudal army took the field.

Meanwhile, who was minding the land? Obviously, fighting men who spent a lot of time assisting their lords, training for war, and schooling their horses could not also be farmers. Obviously, too, the non-warriors of the neighborhood were often in dire need of protection in post-Carolingian times. The solution has been called manorialism, though it is closely bound up with feudalism. The peasants lived on those estates of the lords and vassals, and in return for protection and a place to live and farm they cared for the land and produced the food. Some of it was theirs, and the rest went to the lord and his family. These peasants, known as serfs, were not allowed to leave the land.

The feudal/manorial system, at both top and bottom, could be a brutal affair of thugs fighting each other and brutalizing the peasants. It would have been much worse were it not for the Church. Early on, relations between lords and vassals were ingeniously Christianized. Lord and liegeman swore solemn oaths in the presence of clergy to defend and support each other; young men about to become knights kept a solemn night vigil in church and swore to protect the clergy, the poor, and the weak, and not to harm their property (the Peace of God.) The Truce of God actually limited the times when fighting could be done, and finally eliminated most private wars altogether.

As for the peasants, the Church championed their rights and supported the creation of manorial courts in which a serf might challenge the actions of his lord. (This strikes me as a stunning example of the beneficent effects of Christianity at the lowest level of society; I know of nothing like this kind of legal recourse for the lower classes in the ancient world.) Were the cards often stacked in favor of the lord and against the hapless serf? Undoubtedly. Still, the concept of justice due to every individual was recognized, and it was the Church that insisted upon it.

THE RISE OF TOWNS

By the eleventh century, the agricultural revolution had increased the number of superfluous serfs who yearned to set up shop in the local village. Remember that they were not supposed to leave their lord's estate. Those villages, however, were becoming — for the first time since the fall of the Western Empire — actual towns. They were increasingly large, organized, and self-governing — and they proved irresistible to ambitious and talented serfs. The feudal lords huffed and puffed over the situation; they wanted to control the towns, but they were often outside their jurisdiction and frequently too tough to storm. They wanted to ride in and drag their disobedient serfs back home by their heels, but the town fathers made that a far from simple proposition. There was an expression, "Town air makes free," and it became the custom that if a man could support himself in a town for a year and a day, he was no longer a serf but a free citizen.

The handwriting was on the walls of the castles: the growth of town life was the death knell of feudalism. The system that had got Europe through the last years of the Dark

Ages had outlived much of its usefulness by the eleventh century. True, the ethos, chivalric culture, titles, lord-peasant relationship, and other feudal trappings would long survive, but the days of serfdom were numbered, and there would soon be examples of feudal lords voluntarily freeing their serfs. These bustling new towns, with their new middle class, would become the centers for schools, as well as guilds.

The guild, in fact, can be taken as a metaphor for the Catholic mentality that informed the Middle Ages. Briefly, guilds were organizations of masters and apprentices in the various crafts: shoemakers, butchers, bakers, and so on. When an apprentice could produce work judged, by the guild, worthy of a master (the "masterpiece"), he himself became a master, and had to abide by the detailed regulations of the guild. These were profoundly influenced by Catholic principles.

- The guildsman had to charge the customer a just price, and deliver a quality product.
- The guildsman agreed to limited hours of work and just compensation for himself and his workers.
- Guildsmen were required to assist any of their members who fell ill or were injured, including relieving family members watching over a patient; guilds also came to provide accident insurance and other benefits.
- Every guild had its own patron saint, and celebrated his feast day with a special Mass and solemn procession.
- Guilds contributed to the support and artistic decoration of the local church, and provided for the schooling of talented young men.

Guilds have been accused of creating monopolies, since only guild members could have shops in the towns and their number was limited. But they also enforced standards of quality, just prices and working conditions, and charity. The guild became so much the model for medieval corporate life that the term was applied to purely charitable groups, to the universities when they emerged, and to other enterprises.

THE ROLE OF THE KINGS

How were the new towns able to withstand the opposition of the feudal aristocracy? They appealed to the kings. The emergence of national kings all over Europe was a feature of this springtime; it meant the reappearance of central political authority and the hope of peace and order in every nation. The trouble was that royal rights were contested by the powerful feudal nobility, and the kings were forced to seek allies outside the feudal system.

Among these allies was the new middle class of the new towns: in return for a charter from the king and his protection, a town gave him its allegiance. The richer and more powerful the town, the more valuable this cooperation was between middle class and monarch — and the more the increasingly outdated sway of the country warlord was weakened.

The eleventh century produced admirable kings, beginning in the very year 1000, with the coronation of St. Stephen as king of Hungary with a crown sent by Pope St. Sylvester II. Those pagan Magyars who had wreaked so much havoc on Europe in the tenth century had not only settled down and founded one of the great nation-states of central Europe, they had also produced a royal family that could eventually count some twenty-six of its members as canonized saints or blesseds. (Stephen and his son were both canonized, while his wife was beatified.)

In other countries outside the original core of the Roman and Carolingian empires — in places like Poland, Russia, Scandinavia, and even Iceland — paganism was giving way to Christianity. In the year 1000, Leif Erickson was on his way to North America, and it is intriguing to imagine what we would have become had the Catholic Norse set up permanent colonies here.

Within the European "core," the great Capetian dynasty had begun in France, and the German emperor Henry II would later be canonized. His successor Henry III was wholeheartedly dedicated to Church reform. Under Popes St. Leo IX and St. Gregory VII, the liberation of the Church, including papal elections, from lay control, and the suppression of the great moral evils that had afflicted the clergy were accomplished. Saints were found everywhere: in the papacy, on royal thrones, and in monasteries, schools, and bishoprics.

By the end of the century, Europe had become so powerful and so Catholic that it was able to mount a major international military offensive against its archenemy, Islam, and launch the first (and only successful) Crusade. Of course, not all of this happened at once, and there were periods of famine, anarchy, and corruption as in any other age. But by the end of the eleventh century, Europe's spring had definitely arrived.

THE VIEW FROM GROUND LEVEL

I had got this far in sketching the glories of the eleventh century when I realized that this view, while true, also involves a certain distortion. In the "macro-history" of survey courses and historical summaries, we grow accustomed to the big picture: the Cluniac reform of the tenth century became the great Gregorian reform of the eleventh; the new Catholic nation-states, the economic upturn, the emergence of town life, and the formation of schools, guilds, and other institutions were all positive achievements of the age, and we view them in the context of what came before and after them. The view from ground level, so to speak, the "micro-history" of the century, is quite different, and perhaps a look at it will prove heartening for us, dwellers in another millennium, a thousand years from that springtime.

If you had lived in the early years of the eleventh century, or indeed during most of its first half, you might have been worried and indignant about the famous teacher and theologian who was creating such a stir with his denial of transubstantiation, in which he persisted even after his condemnation, and about that nasty Manichaean sect that was spreading in France and northern Italy, even among the "best" people. Why didn't the Church do something?

You may well have had a parish priest who insisted on recognition for his "wife," whom he claimed to have legally married. His children would be playing outside the church when you arrived for Mass or confession. The neighboring parish was worse; there the priest was a homosexual.

If you took your concerns about the situation to the local monastery, perhaps a daughter-house of Cluny or Gorze, you would be told that indeed the priests were living in sin and scandal, but that they were still validly ordained and were your only recourse for the sacraments. You might consider writing to your bishop, but you knew he had bought his office and was more concerned with his wine cellar and fine horses than conditions in his diocese. Your monastic spiritual adviser would shake his head over the bishop's situation, too, but he would remind you that the bishop could only be dealt with by the pope — reform had to come from the top.

At this, you might, depending on the years in which you lived, be tempted to despair. The morals of at least one of the eleventh-century popes were among the worst in history, while many others were simply content to let things go. Some were the creatures of Roman political factions, and some were beholden to the German emperors. Some popes in the early part of the century actually tried to get reforms implemented, but met with so much indifference or outright resistance that they gave up.

The magnitude of the reforms so badly needed in both the Church and Christian society must have seemed overwhelming and even impossible to a discouraged layman of the time. It was not enough that great reforming monasteries had emerged, or that the saints who headed them, and the saints who came to the thrones of nations, and the saints who preached from many pulpits all lived and worked for the spread of reform: reform in society, in clerical morals, in papal elections, and in lay interference with the Church. Reform had to come from the top. It also, however, had to be able to depend on cooperation all the way to the bottom.

Some recent writers on the Gregorian reform have noted the importance of the gradual growth of a general sentiment — among monks, rulers, and the laity — of exactly what was wrong in the Church and a desire to support the rooting out of the evil. It is perhaps too much to speak of public opinion in the eleventh century — they were not addicted to polls that invited one and all to express their "feelings" about things — but somehow a groundswell of indignation, a consciousness of what needed to be done, was there when the papacy was ready to act. There were even cases of laymen resorting to violence against corrupt clergy, and of bishops urging the laity to reject priests who had bought their ordinations.

There were also a few outstanding figures, both clerical and lay, who stood by the reforming popes and helped them to the end: St. Peter Damian is one example of a fearless cleric who fought corruption with fiery words and fearless counsel. His attack on sodomy is such a devastatingly blunt work that Daniel-Rops remarks, "No decent person could undertake a translation of Peter's *Liber Gomorrhianus*." That it was so badly needed is a judgment on the sins of the times. Countess Matilda of Tuscany, friend and tireless ally of Pope St. Gregory VII, is another influential and attractive figure, and there are many more.

PROSPECTS FOR REFORM

When you ponder it, the fact that so many of the laity, in particular, began to clamor for reform is extraordinary. They were demanding, in effect, that life should be made harder rather than easier — surely not something often seen in human affairs. After all, the corrupt clergy were products of their own society — it was not that they alone were morally corrupt; the laity were, too.

Furthermore, as long as anyone could remember, priests had been "married," and at all levels of clerical life it was the ordinary thing to buy your office and be humbly submissive to the lord/emperor/local thug who granted it to you. It was a kind of miracle that so many monasteries — some like Cluny, established by pious laymen — had for decades been insisting on holiness of life. But it was another thing for large numbers of lay people and regular clergy and bishops to begin to insist that things should change.

The point is that it all had to come together: the reformed monasteries, the emergence of reforming bishops and preachers, the concerned and increasingly indignant laity, and finally (yes, finally!) a saintly pope (St. Leo IX) who got the ball really rolling in mid-century, and another (St. Gregory VII) who kept the momentum going to the end. I cannot refrain from remarking that St. Leo's method was to travel all over Europe, not to hold mass gatherings where people could celebrate themselves, but to call councils where he laid out no-nonsense reform legislation and excommunicated those who would not accept it.

Even if you were fortunate enough to live during the pontificate of St. Leo or St. Gregory, things might have appeared to get worse instead of better. Both died in distressing circumstances, one just released from captivity, the other in exile, after their dealings with the turbulent and brutal Normans of southern Italy backfired. Leo's imprisonment by the Normans was an unfortunate factor in the finalizing of the schism between the Eastern and Western Churches in 1054.

Once set in motion, however, by these powerful and saintly popes, with the assistance of their dedicated lay and clerical allies, there was no stopping the liberation of the Church from lay control or the stamping out of simony and the enforcement of orthodoxy and clerical celibacy. By the middle of the century, those movements were underway, and by the end of the century they were a reality.

I don't know about you, but this gives me no end of hope. If the second millennium had its springtime, why shouldn't the third? We have already seen the emergence of new reform orders and monasteries in our time, and we certainly have an increasing number of informed and educated laity who are fed up with the laxity and doctrinal drift within the Church. We may not see many saints in action right now, but in the 1000s most of them were in monasteries (like the Fátima seer Sister Lucia and the stigmatic St. Padre Pio in our time) or otherwise modestly occupied with the duties of their state in life until their hour came. Ours will come, too; the only question is when.

FOOD FOR THOUGHT

Are there any comparisons one could make between the Church of the eleventh century and the Church today? What are some of the similarities and differences, and what signs of hope do you see for the Church in our time?

READING SUGGESTIONS

This is one of the most difficult periods for which to recommend good books for the general reader. There are numerous scholarly studies in several languages, but general Catholic works on the Church in the early Middle Ages have their difficulties. This is not at all the fault of their authors (I am thinking of Henri Daniel-Rops' **The Church in the Dark Ages** [1959 edition republished by Phoenix Press, 2001] and **Cathedral and Crusade** (E. P. Dutton, 1957), as well as Warren Carroll's **The Building of Christendom** [Christendom College Press, 1987], all recommended), but there is just too much going on at the same time.

Any survey is forced to move from the stirring career of the Cid in Spain to the struggle of St. Stephen with the pagans in Hungary, to the arrival of the Normans in Italy, to the struggle between Pope St. Gregory VII and King Henry IV (including Henry's penitential drama at Canossa), to the spread of Christianity to Scandinavia and Iceland. And that is only part of it.

Much was happening in Russia, Poland, and England, too. The result is that the reader's eyes are apt to glaze over as the multitude of trees causes him to wonder where the forest is.

In such a situation, it may be best to skim some general Church histories and then read the biographies of one or two important figures of the century.

Some of the articles in the old *Catholic Encyclopedia*, available online, are extremely well written, and invite further exploration of related topics. The articles on St. Peter Damian, St. Anselm of Canterbury, and the other saints of the century can be rewarding reading. The seventh volume of Horace K. Mann's *Lives of the Popes in the Middle Ages* (Trübner and Co., 1925) is also very readable.

Finally, I unearthed from my library a book-sale acquisition that many readers may find appealing, and worth asking your library to get on interlibrary loan. It is *Matilda, Countess of Tuscany*, by Mary E. Huddy (revised edition published by John Long, Ltd., 1910). Yes, it's probably outdated; yes, the author has no known scholarly credentials, though she has obviously utilized the primary sources. What she does have is intelligence, sympathy for her subject, and an engaging writing style that brings the period and many of its key players (Gregory VII, Peter Damian, Henry IV) to life. My copy contains a number of notes penciled in the margins by some previous reader, correcting possible errors of date or place. These seem to be minor, and I recommend this book not for accuracy in every detail but for the evocation of an important period in Catholic history and vivid portrayals of its main characters.

CHAPTER EIGHT

Catholic Thought and Culture in the Early Middle Ages

He knows more than any man I ever saw. We have heard his chatter the whole day.... Words pour from his mouth like water from the Tigris.

— ADEMARUS, IN A POEM SATIRIZING THE EAGER
SCHOLARS OF THE ELEVENTH CENTURY

In introducing the eleventh century in *The Mediaeval Mind*, Henry Osborn Taylor writes, "One might liken the Carolingian period to a vessel at her dock, taking on her cargo, casks of antique culture and huge crates of patristic theology. Then western Europe in the eleventh century would be the same vessel getting under way, well started on the mediaeval ocean."

He also likens the two periods to a schoolboy learning his lessons by heart, not thinking much for himself, and then, having left school with much still to learn, beginning to appreciate more deeply both the classical culture and the Catholic heritage. These are apt comparisons.

The cultural lights of the eleventh century were not the superstars we find in the following period: there is no St. Thomas Aquinas or Dante here. Still, the developments in thought, education, and art of this early springtime certainly built up the foundation for the great renaissance to come after it.

ST. PETER DAMIAN

In Italy, the classical heritage had never really been lost, though it had taken a beating from Late Roman decadence and barbarian incomprehension. Education had never died out there either, and there was a steady demand for teachers of grammar, law, and sometimes other disciplines. Eleventh-century Italian scholars seem to have had a penchant for making verses on all kinds of topics — though they are hardly great poetry — and the surviving correspondence of monks like St. Peter Damian provides evidence of classical training. The monks, however, often distrusted classical literature because of its pagan character.

Peter Damian, for example, described in a fine Latin passage how he had formerly loved Cicero and the classical poets and philosophers, though he came to fear their effect on his soul. Peter was, in fact, so learned in the liberal arts that he became a teacher, until his vocation as reformer of clerical corruption took him away from academic pursuits. (Even then, he often expressed his pungent criticisms of popes and clerics in verse.)

Peter is known as a most stern and unbending foe of corruption and laxity; in a letter to his brother, however, he makes a surprising admission: he has never managed to conquer what he calls "scurrility ... my besetting sin," in spite of all his mortifications.

> When, in the ways of spiritual gladness, I wish to show myself cheerful to the brethren, I drop into words of vanity; and when as it were discreetly for the sake of brotherly love, I think to throw off my severity, then indiscreetly my tongue unbridled utters foolishness. If the Lord said: "Blessed are they that mourn, for they shall be comforted," what judgment hangs over those who not only are slack at weeping, but act like buffoons with laughter and vain giggling. . . . If the Truth says: "Woe unto ye who laugh now, for ye shall mourn and weep," what shall they say upon that awful day of judgment who not only laugh themselves, but with scurrilities drag laughter from their listeners?

Peter's secret is out. The formidably ascetic crusader against corruption and frivolity seems to have *told jokes*. He not only giggled and laughed himself, he made others laugh — and, of course, it makes him a much more human saint. (It must also be said that his letters of direction to people living in the world are full of gentleness, and of counsels that still apply today.)

ST. ANSELM

Another Italian saint and scholar was St. Anselm — later archbishop of Canterbury — who made genuine contributions to theology and philosophy. He seems to have been afflicted with a father so impossibly difficult that soon after the death of his mother he felt he could no longer stay at home. He went north, wandering through France until he discovered the abbey of Bec in Normandy, and settled down to study with the great teacher Lanfranc. There he became a monk, and eventually abbot.

Meanwhile, the Norman Conquest of England had occurred, and Lanfranc had become archbishop of Canterbury, assisting William of Normandy with reorganizing the Church in England. To this position Anselm succeeded during the reign of a most trying king, William Rufus. We will not follow

> **From *Cur Deus Homo*, by St. Anselm:**
>
> Now we have found the compassion of God which appeared lost to you when we were considering God's holiness and man's sin; we have found it, I say, so great and so consistent with his holiness, as to be incomparably above anything that can be conceived. For what compassion can excel these words of the Father, addressed to the sinner doomed to eternal torments and having no way of escape: 'Take my only begotten Son and make him an offering for yourself;' or these words of the Son: 'Take me, and ransom your souls.' For these are the voices they utter, when inviting and leading us to faith in the Gospel."

Anselm into exile in Rome and back again, nor in his disputes with King Henry I and into another period of exile. Anselm died in England, as archbishop of Canterbury, in 1109.

Somehow, amid all this turmoil and the trials of a position for which he did not seem to be really suited, Anselm managed to produce the works that earned him the title of Doctor of the Church, and which are still read and debated today. One is the famous *Prosologium*, in which Anselm develops the ontological proof for the existence of God. More appealing, perhaps, is *Cur Deus Homo*, a theological dialogue between Anselm and a questioner he calls Boso on why God became man. It contains some touching passages reflecting a new focus on the sufferings of Our Lord that would characterize medieval spirituality.

ST. WULSTAN

Before leaving England, we might make the acquaintance of an English monk, St. Wulstan of Worcester. I came across him for the first time while researching this chapter, but he is well worth knowing.

Wulstan was the only English bishop to survive the post-Conquest reorganization of the Church, and had the confidence of both William the Conqueror, whom he supported, and Archbishop Lanfranc. Dom David Knowles writes that "[Wulstan] remained a center of English thought and literature till his death. Only at Worcester do we find the transcription of Anglo-Saxon homilies after 1066; and Wulstan's *Life* by Coleman, written in English, is the last great prose work (exclusive of additions to the *Anglo-Saxon Chronicle*) to be written before English, as a literary language, was submerged, first beneath Latin and then beneath French."

A kind and gentle man, Wulstan was nevertheless a determined reformer. "Above all," Knowles adds, "he loved chastity, and here he was relentless with those of his clergy who, like so many priests in the eleventh century, lived as though married. They must choose, he said, between their women and their churches; they could not have both. In this, it is probably safe to say that Wulstan was clearer in statement and more decisive in action than any other contemporary bishop in England."

There is much more to Wulstan's life, but I will end this brief glance at it with another of his great reforming activities: ending the slave trade between the town of Bristol and Ireland. It seems that young people were being brought to the port from all over England and sold into slavery in Ireland, and even the new Norman rulers of England had not been able to stop it. St. Wulstan went to spend some months near the town, preaching in Bristol every Sunday against the slave trade until he succeeded in stamping it out.

FRENCH SCHOLARS

It is in France that the greatest progress was made in that long and arduous task of assimilating the ancient wisdom that the Carolingians had striven to recover from their books and study in their schools. The century opens, in fact, with a French scholar who became pope: Sylvester II, elected in 999, had been known as Gerbert of Aurillac, one of the best-known scholars of his day. As Henry Osborn Taylor writes in *The Mediaeval Mind*, "Gerbert was the first mind of his time, its greatest teacher, its most eager learner, and most universal scholar." Discussing one of Gerbert's many letters in praise of philosophy, Taylor writes, "Save for the language, one might fancy Cicero speaking." He was much involved in politics and Church affairs, but everywhere — from royal courts to cathedral schools — he promoted learning and good teaching. He taught not only logic, rhetoric, and philosophy, but also astronomy, music, and mathematics — even improving the methods of computing then in use.

If all this sounds a little dull, it was absolutely necessary for further cultural progress. These former barbarians, recently civilized and still living in sporadic turmoil, needed to solidify their mastery of basic academic subjects and methods that the Carolingians had developed.

It was tedious work, to be sure. "The decades on either side of the year 1000 were cramped and dull," Taylor writes. The emphasis in monasteries such as Cluny was on reform rather than learning. I cannot resist quoting Taylor again: "Cluny's abbots had enough to do in bringing the monastic world to decency, without dallying with inapplicable knowledge or the charms of pagan poetry." Still, "a moral ordering of life increases thoughtfulness and may stimulate study. Hence ... the Cluniac reforms, like the earlier reforming movements, affected letters favourably in the monasteries."

A telling example of all things working unto good. It also points up the relationship between morally good living and good thinking — the intellect becomes clouded by impurity and dissipation, but works as it should when the rest of the soul is in order.

One of Gerbert's students, Fulbert, became bishop of Chartres and head of the cathedral school that was to become legendary, both for Fulbert's inspired teaching and for its influence on curriculum development and later education. One student, unfortunately, Berengar of Tours, ended up reasoning himself into heresy. Dialectic could work both ways.

CULTURE IN GERMANY

In Germany, the work of assimilation of the Latin classical and patristic heritage was harder. German scholars were not as much at home in Latin as were the French, whose language was born from Latin, so the workload of the Germans was that much harder and involved much laborious translation. It did proceed, though, especially encouraged by abbots, kings, and Gerbert himself, who, as Pope Sylvester II, was a friend of the young and cultured Emperor Otto III.

Two of the many German scholars of this time are particularly interesting: the nun Hroswitha and the crippled scholar Hermann Contractus.

Hroswitha seems to have been the first poet of Saxony, the first feminine German historian, and quite possibly the first

Christian dramatist. Her plays, written in Latin, deal with dramatic incidents in the lives of heroic virgins or repentant sinners, emphasizing the virtue of chastity and the role of Our Lady as the ideal of her heroines. Interestingly, she consciously imitated the dramatic style of pagan authors like Terence, who celebrated the vices of loose women, while her own plays portray the opposite virtues. Hroswitha was not the only one in her convent of Gandersheim who loved study and reading the Latin classics. She was, in fact, taught by another nun of the same convent, in which there seems to have been a number of sister-scholars.

"Among German scholars of the period," writes Taylor, "one can find no more charming creature than Hermann Contractus, the lame or paralytic."

Blessed Herman's father brought him to the monastery of Reichenau when he was seven. "There he studied and taught, and loved his fellows," Taylor writes, "till his death thirty-four years later. His mind was as strong as his body was weak. He could not rise from the movable seat on which his attendant placed him, and could scarcely sit up. He enunciated with difficulty; his words were scarcely intelligible. But his learning was encyclopaedic.... Evil was foreign to his nature. Affectionate, cheerful, happy, his sweet and engaging personality drew all men's love, while his learning attracted pupils from afar."

Just before his death (he had been suffering greatly from pleurisy), Herman spoke of his admiration for Cicero's *Hort-*

Blessed Herman the Cripple (Hermann Contractus) was widely known throughout Europe for his learning. He was the author of a number of works in prose and poetry, including a treatise on mathematics and a historical chronicle. Much better known are his famous hymns to Our Lady, the *Salve Regina* (Hail, Holy Queen) and the *Alma Redemptoris Mater* (Loving Mother of the Redeemer) — still sung in the Church today, close to a thousand years after Blessed Herman's death.

ensius — a work that St. Augustine had also valued — and then of his joy in, and "unspeakable" desire for, eternal life. What a model for scholars and teachers! His relations with his little world also provide an example of how the Catholics of Christendom treated the handicapped.

Thus the laborious work of mastering both the tools of learning and the contents of the precious books of the past went on all over civilized Europe. The people who cared about learning came from all walks of life; they were popes, kings, archbishops, simple monks and nuns, and laity. Their zeal and study were the indispensable prelude to the great flowering of letters and schools in the following two centuries.

FOOD FOR THOUGHT

Do you think learning, at least some form of it, is in any danger of being lost today? Do we value the heritage of the past enough to study it systematically, as the students of the eleventh century did, and do we study it in the languages in which it was produced? What kinds of knowledge do we value, and what types of study and writing are we really good at? Is it any real loss that modern students find Shakespeare, and even Dickens, too hard to read?

READING SUGGESTIONS

Henry Osborn Taylor's first volume of **The Mediaeval Mind** (London, 1911), from which I have quoted several passages, covers all the major countries of western Europe in this period quite thoroughly. Accounts of several of the more prominent literary figures mentioned in the chapter can also be found online.

For the eleventh-century background of England, particularly the radical changes brought by the Norman invasion, some of the articles in a small collection entitled **The Norman Conquest: Its Setting and Impact,** by Dorothy Whitelock, David C. Douglas, Charles H. Lemmon, and Frank Barlow

(Charles Scribner's Sons, 1966) are of interest. Archbishop Lanfranc and Sts. Anselm and Wulstan are mentioned, though rather briefly.

More interesting to read is a delightful collection entitled *The English Way: Studies in English Sanctity from St. Bede to Newman*, edited by Maisie Ward (Sheed and Ward, 1933; Books for Libraries Press, 1968). The authors represented include G. K. Chesterton, Hilaire Belloc, Christopher Dawson, Dom David Knowles (who wrote the charming chapter on St. Wulstan), Father C. C. Martindale, Maisie Ward, and others. At least half the volume deals with figures of the period covered by the book you are reading; some of them you have already met, and others will turn up in later chapters.

CHAPTER NINE

The Church in the High Middle Ages: The Twelfth Century

It was May when flower and leaf are renewed.
— AMBROSE D'ÉVREUX

The 1100s and 1200s represent the high point of Christendom in many ways. Christianity permeated all of society, and shaped everything from economics to politics. Even the weather cooperated; and although droughts and natural disasters did occur, especially near the end of the period in France, Europe in general seems to have experienced agricultural and commercial prosperity.

This does not mean that everything was perfect. Twelfth-century men were only a few generations removed from barbarism; the shortness of life (a feature of human life until the medical breakthroughs of the nineteenth century) meant that the population was young and often turbulent; there was even a time when the kings of all the major countries were under the age of twenty — a thought that should cause any modern parent of teenagers to blanch and shudder.

Still, saints and sinners alike contributed to make this twelfth century, the first half of the high medieval period, one of great achievement and accomplishment. So much was going on all over Europe, in fact, that we must limit this brief overview to the European heartland — namely, England, France, and the German Empire, with only brief attention to Italy and none to the largely Muslim-ruled Iberian peninsula, with which we will catch up in a later chapter.

We must also keep in mind that eleventh-century developments referred to in the previous chapters were continuing: urban life was reviving everywhere in Europe — and with it, town government, guilds, schools, and large-scale building projects that included castles and cathedrals. Monastic orders were growing and new ones founded, while new and dynamic royal families gave shape to the new nation-states of Europe.

THE CRUSADES

The connections between the early twelfth and late eleventh centuries permit us to use a term employed by recent historians to describe centuries that spill over their hundred-year boundaries at one end or the other with respect to some of their themes: here we will speak of the "long" twelfth century, in order to begin its survey with the Crusades that began at the end of the eleventh.

Many readers may already be aware of the rot that is constantly fed to us, under the guise of history, about the Crusades. As a recent writer has neatly put it: "Christians in the eleventh century were not paranoid fanatics. Muslims really were gunning for them." The goal of the Muslim onslaught after the death of Mohammed was to destroy Christian states, establish Islamic ones in their stead, and then "tolerate" Christians and Jews on onerous terms. The Koran expresses the anti-Christian outlook of Islam in these words: "They [the Christians] take their priests and their anchorites to be their lords beside Allah. And [they take as their Lord] Christ the son of Mary; yet they were commanded to worship but One God; there is no God but He" (9:31).

Understandably, the victims of such unprovoked attacks in both Eastern and Western Christendom resisted being conquered, and when they had the necessary means and strength they fought back. Hence, the Crusades. In my classroom lectures, I define the Crusades (here capitalized, to distinguish those against the Seljuk Turks from later enterprises also called "crusades") as, in the first place, multinational military expeditions to assist the Byzantine Empire in combating Islamic aggression and to recover the Holy Land for Christianity. They were not fanatical attempts to force conversions, nor were they early examples of Western colonialism, capitalist ventures, racist rampages, or anything else. Why we should apologize for them is beyond me.

The background is simple: Arabs had conquered Jerusalem and many of the holy places, formerly under Byzantine control, in the first wave of their Great Conquest in the 700s. At the time, the West was too weak to offer military help to the Byzantines, and it had its own struggles against Muslim attacks on Spain, Italy, and France. The Arabs had sometimes proved tolerant and considerate of the Catholic pilgrims who journeyed in surprising numbers to the Holy Land even in the Dark Ages, and many historians have claimed that it was only with the expansion of the Seljuk Turks into Palestine that pilgrims were badly treated.

This turns out to be untrue. There are fascinating contemporary accounts of a large, unarmed group of German pilgrims who went to the Holy Land in 1064, and were attacked by the Arabs and forced to fight for their lives. (Even then, however, many of the pilgrims had scruples about fighting while on a religious expedition and refused to defend themselves.) After many grim adventures, some two thousand out of the original group of seven thousand returned home.

Einar Joranson, who researched and wrote about this "great German pilgrimage," remarks that "to say that 'as long as the Arabs held Jerusalem the Christian pilgrims from Europe could pass unmolested' is to ignore or impugn well-established facts. That the pilgrims did *not* pass unmolested in the third quarter of the eleventh century is proved.... The truth is that maltreatment of pilgrims in Palestine antedated, by many years, the Seljuk occupation of that land." He calls what happened to the poor Germans "the most flagrant example on record of the persecution of occidental Palestine pilgrims prior to the crusades. Perhaps such persecution did not of itself generate the crusading idea; but ... it became one of several pretexts for the crusades and was employed, even in the Clermont address of Pope Urban II, as argument in justification of a military offensive against Islam...."

By the late eleventh century, not only had the Arabs been replaced by the Seljuk Turks, who used even more harassment and violence against pilgrims, but their increasing threats to the very existence of Byzantium came at a time when Europe was in a position to send help. Hence the Byzantine emperor's S.O.S. to Pope Urban II, and the pope's call on the warriors of Europe in 1095 to respond with an army to help the emperor and liberate the Holy Land.

The response to the pope's appeal was the First Crusade — the only successful one — which managed to take Jerusalem in 1099, only to lose it again in the following century. From then until 1270, there would be several more attempts to recover the Holy Land, none of them successful — and papal hopes that military aid would help heal the schism between East and West did not materialize.

THE SIEGE OF JERUSALEM

Much has been made of crusader atrocities, mostly focused on the 1099 capture of Jerusalem (no mention is made of atrocities on the other side). This is due to the graphic descriptions by the chroniclers of the terrible slaughter of the inhabitants, and of horses wading in blood up to their knees.

It was indeed an atrocity, and thousands of innocent people died. It does not exculpate the crusaders, but it does allow us to understand such a horrible deed if we consider that they were at the limit of their endurance, half-starved and badly dehydrated, and that the defenders of Jerusalem engaged in systematic mockery of Christianity. When the crusaders went in procession around the walls of the city, the Muslims accompanied them along the walls, taunting them and carrying crosses which they defiled and insulted.

It may be that at least one of the Christian commanders (possibly Tancred) tried to restrain his men — he did save about three hundred Muslims who had taken refuge on the mosque roof, though other crusaders slew them later. But there was no unified command and no restraints on most of the groups of besiegers. (Some Syrian Christians saved themselves in the Church of the Holy Sepulcher by chanting the *Kyrie Eleison* as the soldiers approached.)

Atrocious it still was, but it ill behooves anyone of our time to point the finger at the crusaders as if we had no My Lai, or — worse — as if we did not incinerate (in cold blood, not in a temporary aberration in the heat of battle) tens of thousands of noncombatants in Dresden and other cities during World War II, or hundreds of thousands in Hiroshima and Nagasaki. The crusaders would have been appalled at us.

THE ASSASSINS

An interesting sidelight to the story of the Crusades is that it provided Westerners with their first encounters with the original "suicide bombers": the Assassins.

This was a sect of a sect of Islam — Ismailism — that developed within the Shiite faction in Persia, Arabia, and North Africa. The Ismailites were said to practice *Taqiyya*, dissimulation of one's identity and beliefs. It took a sinister turn in the eleventh century under the leadership of an extraordinary man called Hasan-e Sabbah — the Osama bin Laden of his day — a convert to militant Ismailism. From his headquarters in a formidable castle in Persia, one of his several strongholds, he taught young men religion, combat techniques, languages, the art of disguise, and of course, *Taqiyya*, before sending them out to kill his enemies. They were not to fail in such assignments, even if it meant their deaths — which it often did because of the boldness of their attacks.

According to Marco Polo, Hasan (or perhaps a Syrian follower, sometimes called "the Old Man of the Mountain" in legends) would drug young men with hashish (a possible derivation of "assassin" or "hashishim" comes from the name of the drug), and have them carried into a secret garden full of exotic sensual delights. When they later came to their senses, back in the grim barracks of the castle, he would tell them they had seen Paradise, where they would go if they died "martyrs" in the assignments he gave them.

Between 1092, when the first religiously motivated murder occurred, and 1256, many kings, viziers, and other enemies of Hasan were killed, as well as some Crusaders. The main enemies of the Assassins, though, were the Seljuk Turks, who, under the leadership of Saladin, were attempting to suppress them. Since the Crusaders and the Assassins were both fighting the Seljuks, Europeans soon ceased to be targets.

One of the terrorizing tactics practiced by the Assassins was the use of warnings they sometimes gave. So skilled were they at disguise that they could infiltrate almost anywhere without suspicion, and many an enemy of their leader awoke to find his room empty but an Assassin dagger or threatening note on his pillow, an unnerving experience. Saladin himself seems to have been the target of this approach. One night he awoke to find a poisoned dagger, a written threat, and some hot breads that only Assassins made on his bed. Believing that the Old Man of the Mountain himself had visited him while he slept, the great Seljuk leader lost his nerve and called off hostilities with the sect. An article by Iyer Pico, published in *Smithsonian* magazine, sums up what Hasan had discovered: "The Assassins discovered that, with a single carefully planned blow, a tiny force prepared to die in the course of killing others could cripple a Goliath of an enemy. They realized, too, that the fear or memory of such an attack could be as paralyzing as an attack itself."

What Pico wrote in 1986 about the Assassins is eerily descriptive of the effects of suicide bombings today.

THE ARCHBISHOP AND THE KING

To return to Europe, we can first survey England in the twelfth century, keeping in mind that it had been taken over by the Normans — originally Vikings — who invaded from Normandy, on the coast of France, in 1066. For the first thirty-five years of the twelfth century, Henry I worked to provide order, peace, and legal justice for his people. There was some friction between Church (St. Anselm) and state (Henry) over lay control of ecclesiastical affairs; it was ironed out between them, but it was an omen of the tragedy to come.

Following Stephen I and a period of struggle for the succession, the grandson of Henry took the throne: Henry II, Plantagenet. Henry made many contributions to England's governmental system, administration, and — especially — legal system, but his reign was also marked by turmoil. Some of the turmoil he imported when he married Eleanor of Aquitaine; some he created himself with the ultimately tragic affair of St. Thomas Becket, another round in the struggle of the state to control the Church.

Thomas Becket was born in 1118 and educated in England and Paris. After working as a financial clerk, he advanced to a position with Archbishop Theobald of Canterbury. Becket was tall, handsome, well mannered, and charming, as well as intelligent. He was known for his generosity and purity of life, as well as his enjoyment of good living and the pomp, banquets, and entertaining that went with his position.

At the age of thirty-six, Becket was recommended by the archbishop as chancellor to twenty-four-year-old King Henry II, whose close friend and mentor he became. He was Henry's companion in both work and leisure, and even on military expeditions. As his wealth increased, so did his lavish entertainments, fine clothes, and other possessions, although he still led a morally blameless life and would not tolerate bad language or behavior in his presence. (So far he is a comfortable kind of saint — a man who knows how to have a good time and still be a decent fellow.)

Very abruptly, it seems, Becket's life and personality were to undergo a great change. Theobald died, and Henry decided to arrange for his friend to become archbishop of Canterbury in 1162. Henry was chagrined to find that Becket was not pleased and grateful when he learned of the king's plans. At first Becket joked, asking the king how the fine brocade he was wearing would suit a shepherd of souls. Becoming serious, he then warned Henry that their friendship would not survive this change in their relations. However, Henry was insistent. Despite the protests of some of the clergy at the appointment of such a worldly man to the highest position in England next to that of the king, Becket was ordained priest and consecrated as archbishop of Canterbury three days later.

Within months, Becket's very appearance, as well as his behavior, had altered: he was gaunt with fasting, wore a hair shirt constantly, slept on a bare pallet or the floor, took "the discipline" (flagellation for self-mortification), and prayed fervently with flowing tears — "as one changed," writes Amy Kelly, "by a miracle of grace." His dinners were still sumptuous for his guests, as befitted his rank, but he himself no longer touched the delicate food. He dedicated himself to the spiritual and temporal needs of his people with the energy he had formerly brought to affairs of state. He insisted on ancient property and legal rights of the Church that the kings had long been accustomed to exercise, and demanded the Church's rights in little as well as in great things.

The inevitable conflict with Henry, whose maniacal rages were often provoked by his archbishop's intransigence, Becket's years of exile, the wishy-washiness of the pope — now supporting Becket, now undermining him — the semi-reconciliations of the two old friends, make for a tangled and confused tale that often wearies the reader. The greatest chess player in England now thought no more of games or jokes but dedicated himself heart and soul to the defense of the rights of the Church in a fierce and unbending stance.

The final act is well known: how Henry, in a rage again, let slip a fervent wish to be rid of the troublesome prelate; how four of his knights took him at his word and, on December 29, 1170, cut down Becket in his cathedral as he faced them bravely, seeming to have already had a vision of just where the blows would smite him. The profusion of miracles at the tomb and Henry's public penance there marked both the triumph of Becket and the birth of one of the greatest pilgrimage sites in the West. (Given the trouble and humiliation Becket had caused the crown, it is not surprising that in the sixteenth century Henry VIII, in another Henrician rage, would have the remains of St. Thomas Becket disinterred and scattered to the winds.)

Henry II was succeeded by his son, Richard the Lionhearted, an absentee monarch with a taste for crusading, jousting, and chivalry, around whom a long-lasting legend soon developed. The century ended with the accession of another of Henry's sons, bad King John, whom we will meet in another chapter.

ELEANOR OF AQUITAINE

A few words about Eleanor, though no few words can do her justice. She hailed from the south of France, the granddaughter of a troubadour ruler of the Duchy of Aquitaine. Unhappily married to the French king, she hated the cold north and the bookish character of her spouse; when she went on crusade with him and scandalized the company by her behavior with her young uncle in Antioch, the days of the marriage were numbered. Despite some papal marriage counseling, the couple obtained an annulment on grounds of consanguinity.

Within weeks, as Eleanor was returning south to Aquitaine, the future Henry II came to meet her and apparently won her heart — as well as her dowry of Aquitaine. He may have soon regretted it. Eleanor was as headstrong as he was. By the time the several sons she gave him (instead of the daughters she had given Louis of France) were teenagers, they were taking her part against their father. At one point, Henry shut her up in a castle, from which her sons rescued her. The whole story reads like a soap opera, but this is a book about culture, not soap, so we will skip the interesting details.

To her credit, Eleanor was intelligent, an able regent for her son Richard during his lengthy absence from the kingdom, and a pious benefactor of the Church. She was particularly fond of the abbey of Fontevrault in Normandy, which she often visited and to which she may have retired to spend her last days. She was blessed with a long life, and at the age of eighty took a matchmaking trip through France and across the Pyrenees to find a bride for one of her grandsons. She died at the age of eighty-two and is buried in her beloved abbey.

THE KINGDOM OF FRANCE

In France, meanwhile, the main problem of the French kings was extending their authority beyond the small area around Paris that they directly controlled. The rest of the country was largely in the hands of feudal lords, among whom, thanks to the marriage of Eleanor and possession of the Duchy of Normandy from which they originated, were the kings of England. The process of both working within and weakening the feudal system gradually enabled France to become unified under the rule of a long series of competent and pious kings, though it took both diplomacy and warfare with the English to accomplish it.

Louis VI worked to consolidate royal power in the beginning of the century, and his son Louis VII continued it. This poor Louis might have become a cleric had his elder brother not died, with the result that he became heir to the throne and acquired Eleanor — whom he seems to have really loved. He was not the most practical or forceful of the French kings, but he had the advice of the great Abbot Suger; he was honorable and well-meaning; and he left a prosperous and orderly state to his great son, Philip II, Augustus, who reigned into the following century where we will meet him.

THE HOLY ROMAN EMPIRE

Unlike the kings of England and France, who generally concentrated on developing harmonious and strong nation-states, the kings of Germany thought big. To them belonged the title of Holy Roman Emperor, and they tended to take it literally. What's a Roman Empire without Rome? Why shouldn't they, in fact, restore the original empire so as to scoop in France, England, and points south and east?

Their desire to control at least Italy was one of their immediate goals. Another was to control their own feudal lords, who were more powerful than their counterparts in France since they ruled large blocs of what had been the old Carolingian Empire. A third goal was to control the Church in Germany through lay investiture, largely because of the prime real estate administered by bishops who were also feudal lords. The achievement of all these goals simultaneously was impossible, but that didn't stop the kings from trying.

Time after time a German king would tramp over the Alps into Italy with his army and battle the Italians into submission, while back home the feudal lords mounted a revolt against him. Back he would go to deal with the domestic revolt, while in Italy the Italian cities shook off German rule. At the same time, he was generally at loggerheads with the ruling pope and periodically excommunicated because of his attempts to control the Church. These wars, Italian and civil, together with royal crusades and the constant struggle with the Church, combined to keep the German situation unstable and Germany disunited. Near the end of the twelfth century, a German king would make a fateful marriage that would have appalling consequences for both his country and the Church, as we will see in the thirteenth century.

THE PAPACY

The twelfth-century papacy saw the continuation of the Gregorian reform movement; King Louis VI of France abandoned lay investiture early in the century, and Archbishop Anselm got it forbidden in England.

As we have seen above, the Germans were a different proposition. Emperor Henry V actually kidnapped Pope Paschal II and the cardinals in the course of a meeting in Rome intended to resolve the investiture issue. After two months' imprisonment, Paschal's will was broken and he granted lay investiture. Outcry within the Church forced him to retract it, and Rome soon saw Henry again. Pascal died, his successor took refuge at Cluny, and Henry set up an anti-pope. Thus it went until the Concordat of Worms brought temporary peace: it included compromise in some details, but victory for the Church in the abandonment of lay investiture by the emperor.

The rest of the century saw more troubles with the Germans, particularly the great Frederick Barbarossa, more antipopes, and a revolution in Rome. At the end, however, in the year 1198, one of the greatest popes of all time stepped into the pages of history.

FOOD FOR THOUGHT

Is there any possibility today that the West as a whole might again launch a Crusade? What conditions would have to be met for an international force to take the field against Muslim powers? To what extent do the wars against Afghanistan and Iraq resemble the Crusades?

Can you think of any bishop-martyrs — or bishop-confessors — of the twentieth or twenty-first centuries who can be compared with St. Thomas Becket? (Think of China and Eastern Europe under communism.) Is the Church today anywhere subject to pressure by hostile governments as it was in England, the Holy Roman Empire, and even Italy in the Middle Ages? What types of influence are brought to bear upon the papacy and local hierarchies in modern times?

READING SUGGESTIONS

On the Crusades, there are numerous valuable works: the English translation of Régine Pernoud's **The Crusaders** was reprinted by Ignatius Press in 2003. It is not so much a chronological history as a series of essays on various aspects of the Crusades and those who participated in them. (Anything by Pernoud is well worth reading.)

In 1937, Hilaire Belloc wrote **The Crusades**, a short work that Tan Books reprinted in 1992. I am not an unqualified admirer of Belloc as a historian, though most of his works make for interesting reading. In this one, he expresses some novel points of view and interpretations that are worth considering.

A valuable and fascinating collection of primary documents can be found in *The First Crusade: The Chronicle of Fulcher of Chartres and Other Source Materials*, edited by Edward Peters (University of Pennsylvania Press, 1971, 1998). This includes eyewitness accounts of many incidents in the First Crusade; the various views of the same event — an example is the several differing versions of Pope Urban II's famous summons to the Crusade — are interesting to read and compare.

You can't beat Harold Lamb for page-turning popular history. In *The Crusades: Iron Men and Saints* (first published in 1930 by Doubleday, Doran & Co.), he has certainly utilized the primary sources and produced an extremely readable account — and the notes are as interesting as the text.

On Eleanor of Aquitaine, the best study is Amy Kelly's *Eleanor of Aquitaine and the Four Kings*, (Vintage Books, 1957; Harvard University Press, 1974). The whole drama of the turbulent Plantagenets is there, engagingly written, including one of the best accounts of the conflict between Henry II and Thomas Becket.

CHAPTER TEN

Catholic Thought and Culture in the Twelfth Century

It is only through symbols of beauty that our poor spirits can raise themselves from things temporal to things eternal.
— Abbot Suger

The nun who taught me medieval history in college used to compare the twelfth and thirteenth centuries in this way: When is a rose most perfect? Is it when it is in its fullest bloom, just before its petals fall to the ground? Or is it when it is a bud, just beginning to open?

The comparison is telling. The thirteenth has been called "the greatest of centuries," and as a Thomist and researcher in that spectacular period I would never deny its grandeur. It is also true, however, that the signs of decay were already apparent by the end of that century, as we will be seeing in the next two chapters.

The twelfth century, on the other hand, has all the charm of June, when things in nature are fresh and new, and there is so much of summer ahead. It is a refreshing time to visit.

In considering the culture of the "long twelfth century," we find that many of its major figures, such as Abelard and St. Bernard, were actually born in the eleventh century, while a number of the great achievements of the time had their roots in the previous period. Still, so many new developments gathered momentum in the twelfth century, and so many vivid personalities appeared on its stage, that the term "Twelfth-Century Renaissance" is no exaggeration.

From the start, the Church had fostered learning and the careful collecting of books in libraries. All through the Dark

Ages, as we have seen, books were copied and gathered together, and here and there some few scholars were able to read and understand them. I recall the words of a self-taught author from a poor family in San Francisco in the 1950s, who recounted how his father once showed him the family's small book collection and told him, "There is gold in the books."

Dark Age copyists, scholars, and students knew that, and had a great reverence for books. They lacked, however, the systematic instruction and, often, the leisure, to mine all the gold in their books and make full use of it. By the twelfth century, the time had come.

EDUCATIONAL DEVELOPMENT

An organized system of higher education was vital to the process. Charlemagne had ordered churches and monasteries to set up schools, and the process continued despite the tenth-century upheavals and invasions. By the eleventh century, we find numerous cathedral schools that by the twelfth century will be famous for their teaching and curricula, as well as for their great teachers (including Abelard, probably the most flamboyant). The end of the century will see the beginning of universities in the modern sense. Scholars were now using the treasures in the books creatively: once they were capable of understanding and mastering them, they could take the ideas they found and apply them in new ways.

LITERATURE AND ART

There was movement in so many cultural areas that it would take many volumes to discuss them fully. Vernacular literature, poetry, drama, history, biography, translations of Greek classics transmitted by the Moors in Latin, the application of Greek philosophical methods to theology, the beginnings of Gothic architecture — there has rarely been a more vibrant and creative time in history. We cannot deal with all of it here — not even with some of the major figures in theology — but we can glimpse at least part of the excitement and glory of it through the eyes of four major personalities: Abelard, St. Bernard of Clairvaux, Abbot Suger of Saint Denis, and Heloise.

They are all French, since France — and to a lesser extent England — was the center of this renaissance.

ABELARD

Master Abelard, born in year 1079, was a superstar of the cathedral schools of his time; students came from everywhere to take his classes in theology and philosophy, and his teaching career reached its height in the schools of Paris. What attracted such interest was his new approach of using the principles of Greek logic — dialectics — to study matters of faith. (St. Thomas Aquinas would use a similar method in the following century, but he was far clearer than Abelard on the necessary distinctions between faith and reason.)

Abelard wrote significant works on ethics, logic, and the vexed question of "universals." His book *Sic et Non* ("Yes and No") examined the problem of apparent contradictions in some of the teachings of the Church Fathers, and proposed solid rules for textual analysis — making sure a text attributed to an author was really his, examining the purpose and intent of legal principles, considering the mode of expression used in a text — and where contradictions remained, he attempted to resolve them. *Sic et Non* also, however, included this statement: "By collecting contrasting divergent opinions I hope to provoke young readers to push themselves to the limit in the search for truth, so that their wits may be sharpened by their investigation. It is by doubting that we come to investigate, and by investigating that we recognize the truth."

Encouraging the young to "doubt," as well as Abelard's bold application of reason to the truths of the Faith, particularly the Trinity, became increasingly controversial.

From *Sin et Non*, by Abelard:

With these prefatory words, it seems right, as we have undertaken to collect the diverse sayings of the Holy Fathers, which stand out in our memory to some extent due to their apparent disagreement as they focus on an issue; this may lure the weaker readers to the greatest exercise of seeking the truth, and may render them sharper readers because of the investigation. Indeed this first key of wisdom is defined, of course, as assiduous or frequent questioning. Aristotle, the most clear-sighted philosopher of all, advised his students, in his preface 'Ad Aliquid,' to embrace this questioning with complete willingness, saying (cited by Boethius, *In Categorias Aristotelis*, ii): 'Perhaps it is difficult to clarify things of this type with confidence unless they are dealt with often and in detail. However, it would not be useless to have some doubts concerning individual points.' And indeed, through doubting we come to questioning and through questions we perceive the truth.

"In consequence of this, Truth herself says (Matthew 7:7), 'Ask and it shall be given you; knock and it shall be opened to you.' Teaching us this spiritual lesson with Himself as an example, He let Himself be found, at about twelve years of age, sitting and questioning in the midst of the teachers, showing Himself to us in the model of a student with His questioning, before that of a schoolmaster in his pronouncements, although His knowledge of God was full and complete. And when some passages of Scripture are brought before us, the more the authority of the Scripture itself is commended, the more fully they excite the reader and tempt him to seek the truth."

ST. BERNARD

St. Bernard of Clairvaux, whom it is time to introduce, called Abelard's theology "foolology," and his relentless opposition eventually got Abelard condemned.

There is too much to tell of Bernard here, because his life, which began in 1090, is chock full of varied and important missions, writings, and endless preaching. It is, in fact, a paradox because Bernard wanted nothing more than to remain hidden in his cell and devoted to prayer; as it turned out, his public days probably far outnumbered his cell days. Even strong suggestions from Rome that he stay in his cell and stop trying to right wrongs that did not concern him failed to stop him.

God certainly had many tasks for Bernard: revitalizing the Cistercian Order; sorting out a painful papal schism; wrangling with his friend, Blessed Peter the Venerable of Cluny; preaching the Second Crusade; advising the pope in often blunt language; writing the rule for the new order of the Knights Templar; and composing wonderful works in mystical theology, particularly on the love of God. He has a reputation for caustic wit, puritanism, and vindictiveness — partly because of his relentless campaign against Abelard — but that is a distorted view. Here is one vignette that shows the tender heart of Bernard, described by Henry Osborn Taylor in *The Mediaeval Mind*.

Bernard's younger brother, Gerard, who had entered the abbey of Citeaux with him, was very dear to Bernard and a great help to him in his work. Rather suddenly he died, still quite young, and Bernard performed the burial service without giving way to visible emotion.

Later, continuing with business as usual, Bernard was proceeding with a series of sermons he had been giving on an Old Testament text and suddenly came to a dead stop. Abandoning his text, he allowed his grief to gush forth in a powerful and poignant torrent: "What have I to do with this Song, who am in bitterness? . . . Grief, suppressed, roots deeper." (Dr. Freud, meet St. Bernard. He understood repression before you did.) "Why did we so love, and now have lost each other! . . . I seem to hear my brother saying: 'Can a mother forget her suckling child; even so, yet will I not forget thee.' That does not help, where no hand is stretched out." And he went on to speak from his heart about Gerard and about his grief. Anyone who has suffered a similar loss can identify immediately with his words in this magnificent and spontaneous address.

As for Bernard's puritanical outlook, it is true that he wanted austerity and simplicity in the decoration of Cistercian churches and chapels. He thought the many decorations, ornate candlesticks, images, symbols, and statues found in Cluniac monasteries to be a distraction that a true monk should not be looking at. A monk should be focused on God, his soul, and the interior rather than the exterior world. After Bernard visited Cluny, he wrote a withering criticism of its abundant artwork, of which he gave a detailed inventory. What is interesting is his seemingly total recall of all the decorations and furnishings of the place; he had been gazing at them, all right, despite his own advice to the true monk, probably more than the Cluniacs themselves did.

THE CONFLICT

Bernard was certainly not insensitive to beauty, but he was intolerant of heresy, schism, and false teaching — and he found dangerous ideas in the teachings of Abelard and his revolutionary student, Arnold of Brescia. He spared no pains to secure the condemnation of Abelard at the Council of Sens in 1141, though he was unable to secure from him the profession of faith he desired. (Abelard did express his devotion to the teachings of the Church in a private letter to Heloise: "I do not wish to be an Aristotle if this means that I must separate myself from Christ.")

Unconvinced that he was wrong, Abelard appealed to Rome. There again he was condemned. He was on his way to Rome to appeal the judgment when he stopped at Cluny. A tired, worn-out man, Abelard received permission from Blessed Peter the Venerable to lodge there. Abbot Peter then accomplished the astonishing diplomatic feats of reconciling Abelard with Bernard, soothing relations with the pope — so that although the specific condemnations were not annulled,

Abelard was permitted to teach at Cluny — and persuading the great teacher to take up residence and teach there.

Here Abelard found peace at last, and from all accounts lived a holy and penitential life until, shortly before his death in 1142, Blessed Peter sent him to the monastery of Saint-Marcel, where he could lead a more calm and restful life than at bustling Cluny.

HELOISE

Where does Heloise come into all this? Here we come to one of the most famous, tragic, and enigmatic love stories in history.

When Abelard was at the height of his popularity in Paris, a canon of the cathedral, Fulbert, in whose house the professor lodged, engaged him to tutor his niece, Heloise. She was about eighteen, and he was nearing forty. The girl already had a reputation for classical learning, and was anxious to learn the new philosophy from the great teacher. What she and Abelard had in common was a great love and admiration for Abelard, and he soon seduced her. By the time her uncle discovered the affair, Heloise was pregnant.

Abelard had her spirited away to the house of his sister, where she gave birth to a son whom they named Astrolabus ("The danger of being the child of a couple of intellectuals," remarks Jacques le Goff). Leaving little Astrolabus with his aunt, they returned to Paris and, after a secret night vigil in a church, were quietly married. Abelard wanted the marriage kept secret so that his professional status would not suffer: he had been tonsured, and though this would not of itself preclude marriage, theology and philosophy professors were supposed to be celibate. Heloise herself pointed out the incompatibility of family life with single-minded dedication to learning.

A secret marriage, however, did not satisfy the honor of Heloise's uncle, since the affair had achieved public notoriety; in the large Parisian student community songs were being sung about the two scandalous lovers. Fulbert therefore publicly announced the marriage; Heloise just as publicly denied it, which led to violent arguments until Abelard sent his wife to a convent for safety. Now Fulbert didn't know what to think. Was Abelard repudiating his wife?

Her family took horrible revenge: one night, while Abelard was asleep, some of them attacked and mutilated him where, as he put it, he had sinned. Gone were his status and reputation now. He became a monk and Heloise a nun — reciting passages from the Roman poet Lucan as she took the veil.

Their correspondence reveals her lasting love for him as her husband, while Abelard would come to address her as the "bride of Christ." She fulfilled all her duties admirably; but while his conversion to a devout spiritual life is evident, hers remains much more of a mystery. She had the burden of surviving her husband by many years, before dying at the same age he did. When Abelard died, Peter the Venerable sent his body to her with a touching letter. "He was yours," he wrote, "before he was ours." They are now buried together.

ABBOT SUGER'S NEW STYLE

While these dramatic events were unfolding and infant universities were growing out of the cathedral schools, spectacular developments were in progress in all the visual arts. The most innovative of the arts in this century of renaissance, however, was one that was not in fact a "rebirth" but the invention of something entirely new: Gothic architecture, the first new architectural style in seven hundred years. It owes its origins to an extraordinary figure of many talents, Abbot Suger of the royal abbey of Saint-Denis, outside Paris.

Suger seems to have been the son of a serf (yes, plenty of social mobility occurred in the Middle Ages). He rose to a high position not only in the Church, but also in the French state as adviser to the king and sometimes as regent, and his whole career is of interest.

What concerns us here is the idea he had about what the inside of a church should be like. Certainly the Romanesque churches are glorious structures, but Suger found them dark. He wanted to open up the walls of the church and fill them with glass to allow the sun to shine through. This one desire led to a whole chain of innovations in design: the Gothic structures soared high into pointed spires, their walls supported from outside, with huge rose windows inserted at various points. The designers then realized that while plain glass let in light, colored glass that depicted biblical and other important events could illuminate not only church interiors but minds as well: the windows became, in fact, the "books" of those who could not read words but could read glass images.

Suger also had the characteristically medieval idea of the importance of beauty, because the beauty perceived by the senses leads the mind to absolute beauty, which is God; beauty, in fact, is something added to things by God to draw our minds to Him. Churches in the new style, including the great cathedral of Chartres, were at that time increasingly dedicated to Our Lady, and some of the loveliest statues ever produced depict her smiling — a new departure that would not survive the high medieval period, in which there was so much to smile about. The full development of the Gothic lies in the future, and we will examine perhaps its most appealing example in the next chapter.

If you go to Paris you will no doubt visit one of Our Lady's most famous Gothic churches, Notre Dame. After your visit, go to the right from the west door as far as the river and right again along the quay to the east. At number 9 Quai aux Fleurs, you will see a plaque identifying the house as the residence of Heloise and Abelard in 1118, rebuilt in 1849. The neighborhood is very ancient, and maybe it is the house. It's somewhere around there anyway.

FOOD FOR THOUGHT

Do you agree with Heloise and medieval university authorities that a man whose vocation is scholarship should not be burdened with the cares of marriage and family life? In what ways was devotion to philosophy considered to resemble a religious vocation?

If the Gothic cathedral was the epitome of high medieval architecture, what is most typical of twenty-first-century architecture? How do the styles differ?

READING SUGGESTIONS

The Renaissance of the Twelfth Century, by Charles Homer Haskins (Harvard University Press, 1927, 2005), a pioneering American medievalist writing in the 1920s and 1930s, is still eminently readable, as is Henry Osborn Taylor's two-volume *The Mediaeval Mind*. While both these works are partially outdated, they are still worth reading as introductions to the period.

Etienne Gilson's *Heloise and Abelard* (University of Michigan Press, 1960) is a most attractive little book that not only explores the whole story of the couple's lives but also gives excerpts and paraphrases from their correspondence. The paperback edition was first published in 1960 but has since been reprinted several times. Abelard's autobiography, *The Story of Abelard's Adversities*, exists in several editions, sometimes as part of collections of the letters. My edition (The Pontifical Institute of Mediaeval Studies, 1964) includes a valuable introduction by Gilson. It is simply written and very hard to put down; a little masterpiece.

There are many books on St. Bernard, including more than one by Father Bruno Scott James. His *St. Bernard of Clairvaux: An Essay in Biography* (Hodder & Stoughton, 1957) is a short, attractive work that includes Bernard's side of the Abelard affair as well as his relationships with his friends Blessed Peter the Venerable and Abbot Suger.

Pictures are essential for a grasp of the glory of twelfth-century art. Most libraries have books in their art sections on the period, with two being very worthwhile. The first is *The Flowering of the Middle Ages*, by Joan Evans (McGraw-Hill, 1966), which seems to exist in a couple of formats, including a sumptuous, oversized version. (Her commentary is highly opinionated — she calls St. Bernard "a fanatic" — but it is the wealth of illustrations that makes the book valuable). *Art of the Early Middle Ages*, by François Souchal (Harry N. Abrams, Inc., 1968), is one of the high-quality Abrams art books that covers Romanesque and early Gothic art — well worth perusing and perhaps owning.

CHAPTER ELEVEN

The Greatest of Centuries?

This holy man loved God with all his heart, and followed Him in His acts; and this appeared in that, as God died for the love He bore His people, so did the king put his body in peril... for the love he bore to his people.
— JEAN DE JOINVILLE, ON KING ST. LOUIS IX

The thirteenth century was termed "the greatest" in James J. Walsh's 1907 work, *The Thirteenth, Greatest of Centuries*. Though outdated and written by a nonspecialist, the book is still worth reading as an introduction to the period, and for the enthusiasm the author felt for the Catholic civilization he was describing.

Certainly in many ways this century can be compared with the great fifth century B.C. in Athens for creativity and lasting cultural contributions. Its saints are among the greatest: Thomas, Bonaventure, Francis, Dominic, Louis, Elizabeth, Gertrude, and so many more. But why does the Church, in an opening prayer for the feast of the Stigmata of St. Francis, say that in his day "the world was growing cold?" This echoes the remark of St. Francis himself to the effect that in his time (this same glorious century) "Charity had grown cold."

How could that be, in the greatest of Catholic centuries? And how could it be that the century that followed it could be such a disaster in every way, if some bad seed had not been quietly germinating unobserved even as the glory dazzled?

ENGLAND

The opening of the thirteenth century marks a turning point in history in a number of ways. Some years ago the Metropolitan Museum of Art in New York devoted a magnificent exhibit at The Cloisters to "The Year 1200." We will be looking at the cultural glories and theological developments of the century in the next chapter, but here we must look at the European world in 1200.

If we start with England, the picture is not encouraging. Bad King John had come to the throne in 1199 and was busy losing battles — and key Angevin territories — to the French king. He was also busy alienating his subjects, as he had already alienated the Irish he had been sent by his father to govern a few years earlier. Christopher Brooke wrote of him, in *From Alfred to Henry III,* "In fact, John was not much more despotic than his father and brother, but his manners and misfortunes made him appear to be so, and the disasters of his reign encouraged men to resist him to his face."

He was the least favorite son of his mother, Eleanor of Aquitaine, though she did her best to help and advise him until her death. Not even she, however, could rein in his abuses of power that eventually led to the revolt of his barons in 1215 and the extracting of the "Great Charter," Magna Carta, from him.

The significance of this famous document lies mostly in what was made of it in later times as a precedent for limiting (or abolishing) royal authority. At the time, it was no such thing. Many states of the period had similar documents, spelling out what were called the "liberties" of various groups of subjects that the ruler was bound to respect. John's predecessors had also issued charters. Such documents in no way usurped the ruler's authority, though they specified details of its exercise. John's barons were actually excommunicated by the pope, not so much because of the Charter as because of "the manner in which it was extracted" — that is, for rebellion against a legitimate monarch. This is a large and complex issue, and I am glad to be able to tell you that John died the year following his signing of the Charter, so we needn't get into it. A poem in one of the *Winnie the Pooh* books sums up his reign: "King John was not a good man," it begins. Too true.

The long reign of John's young son Henry III, whose interests were protected by the papal legate who advised and supported him, included a period of civil war that was resolved before he died. An interesting feature of that revolt is that at one point both parties took their case to the great St. Louis IX, king of France, for arbitration — such was that monarch's reputation for astute and just decisions, as well as for sanctity. By the end of the century, under Edward I, we find the distinctively English institution of Parliament operating. While other rulers also had advisory councils of citizens from various classes, England's assembly was a *national* one, more suited to an island with a more or less cohesive population than it would have been for other countries.

England ended the century as a unified state with a distinctive national character. Economic growth, increase in trade, population, and income, development of schools and universities, and an unusual number of saintly and competent bishops to govern the Church made thirteenth-century England an attractive place in which to live. (This would be especially true if estimates of how much people worked are correct. I have been unable to verify the claims that a man could earn enough in fourteen weeks of work to keep his family for a year, but certainly the great number of holy days, plus Sundays, made for less work at the same time as the standard of living seems to have risen. This was true of the other major countries, too.)

FRANCE

France in this century went from glory to glory, both in the quality and policies of her kings, defense of the Church against heresy and support for the last Crusades, and the high civilization and economic prosperity that characterized her. Philip II had been ruling for twenty years when the century began, and had already gone on the legendary Third Crusade, the Crusade of the Kings, with Richard the Lion-Hearted of England and Frederick Barbarossa of Germany. That expedition

— though a rich source of anecdotes, legends, and novels — was as unsuccessful as all the Crusades that followed the first.

Philip, however, was definitely a royal success, though his domestic life was not. Historians still puzzle over why, the day after he married the young and pretty Ingeborg of Denmark, he was observed gazing at her with horror during their coronation ceremony, after which he left her and refused to return. She knew no French but she kept repeating, "Roma! Roma!" appealing to the pope for vindication of her rights.

The puzzling business dragged on for years, with Pope Innocent III trying to force Philip to take back his wife, and Philip — sometimes hinting at "sorcery" as the obstacle — refusing to do so. There was a semi-settlement in the end, but meanwhile the king was able to assert royal authority over most of those French lords who had been unwilling to submit to his predecessors, defeat the allies of Bad King John in a significant battle, regain French land lost to the English, and leave to his descendents a powerful state and improved government. In the early part of the century, he, like his successor, also supported the Albigensian Crusade, that target of anti-Catholic propaganda.

THE ALBIGENSIAN CRUSADE

The heresy of the Albigensians (the name comes from the town Albi), and its impact on the mentality of the time, will be discussed in the following chapter. Here we can review some of the facts.

This is the myth about the Albigensian Crusade: Once upon a time there was a romantic, peaceful area in southern France where the sun always shone, people sang songs of courtly love, and were kindly tolerant of differences in opinion and lifestyles — they resembled us, in fact. This utopian region only asked to be left alone, but the evil, rigid, intolerant, and power-hungry Princes of the North would not do that. On the pretext of heresy in the South, they descended on it with their armies, led by bloodthirsty bishops and papal legates, and wiped out the charming culture of the South in a ghastly blood bath. After slaughtering the charming inhabitants, they divvied up the land, which is what they wanted all along.

Here are the facts about the Albigensian Crusade: Catharism was a weird cult that stood for the negation of all Christian teaching as well as all secular authority. As with later heretical movements, it became mixed up with politics: southern lords espoused it as a symbol of their independence from the authority of the French kings, and it brought a certain coherence to the stubborn resistance of the southerners to that authority.

Preaching and "dialoguing" proved futile in checking the spread of the heresy, especially after the murder of a papal legate sent to negotiate with the Cathars. It finally became clear that only armed conquest — a crusade — had a hope of suppressing this most dangerous of sects, and the refusal of the south to submit brought tragedy upon it. (There is no evidence that a papal legate said during a battle, "Slay them all! God will know His own," as is frequently claimed.) The northerners did not divvy up the lands of the south; most of them served in the feudal way for brief periods of a few weeks and then went home. Even the captain-general Simon de Montfort's acquisitions were not permanent. The massacre at Béziers in 1209 was actually provoked by an attack on, not by, the crusaders.

Even with the record set straight and the disinformation corrected, the suppression of Catharism was a brutal and melancholy enterprise, and even then the movement was not wholly erased from history. The French kings ended up with their authority extended over a large area they had not previously controlled, which was in the long run a good thing for France and the Church (this is a point disputed by some historians).

The high point of France's political, cultural, and religious development came with the great St. Louis IX, grandson of Philip. Legendary for his love of justice (we have seen how even rival Englishmen consulted him), a model husband and father, devoted to the welfare of his people, he died on crusade in 1270 — a date generally considered to mark the end of the great enterprise to free the Holy Land and shore up the Byzantine Empire that had begun in 1096. The king also commissioned one of the gems of Gothic architecture, which will be discussed in the next chapter. He left his son the most powerful and prosperous state in Europe, the center of Catholic civilization.

FRED THE AWFUL

In contrast to England and France in the thirteenth century, Germany did not become a nation-state. In fact, it came apart at the seams and stayed that way until its unification in 1871, due to the disastrous policies of the sinister King (and Holy Roman Emperor) Frederick II.

Fred figures prominently in my dissertation as the violent antagonist and persecutor of the dissertation's hero, Pope Gregory IX; I therefore cannot pretend to have much appreciation for his good points, if any. I know too much about his bad points, which were many. He blazed like a comet through the political atmosphere of his time, the most flamboyant, fierce, and unconventional monarch in a century liberally strewn with flashy characters. When he finally fizzled out, after a career that seemed too short for his fervent supporters and endless to his enemies, Germany was left in pieces. Not that he intended things to turn out that way; when they did, far from blaming Fred, his countrymen wistfully invoked a legend that had him merely sleeping in a cave somewhere, soon to return and sort things out.

Fred was known to his contemporaries as *stupor mundi* (the wonder of the world). Popes Gregory IX and Innocent IV wondered why he had to turn up during their reigns; northern Italians wondered when he would swoop down again on their towns and start taking and torturing hostages; the king of Scotland wondered why his daughter had disappeared so completely following her marriage to Fred; his Muslim friends, seeing him dressed like an Eastern potentate and traveling with a harem, wondered why he didn't convert to Islam. As for his three wives, poor things, they must have wondered... but that does not come into this story.

The calamity that was Fred began with the marriage of his parents at the end of the previous century. Henry VI, king of Germany (and, later, also Holy Roman emperor), married Constance, Norman heiress of the Kingdom of Sicily, which included the southern half of Italy. To calm Italian and papal fears of a German-Sicilian mega-state, Henry agreed that Sicily and Germany would never be ruled by the same king. Whereupon he died, shortly followed by his wife, leaving Frederick a three-year old orphan. When Frederick was five, a German warlord trying to kidnap him was startled to find himself attacked by the child, who fought him fiercely, tearing the warlord's skin and clothes. The archbishop of Capua, describing the incident to the pope, concluded that if only Fred could live to grow up he would amount to something big. Pope Innocent, whom Constance had asked to be her son's protector, exerted what pressure he could on a series of "guardians." One imagines that they were all tempted to murder their unruly captive, but somehow they restrained themselves, and Fred duly came of age (all of fourteen) in 1208.

There were rumors of his ungovernable temper and unpleasant games. It may not have been true that precocious scientific curiosity led him to cruel "experiments" on living creatures, but no one who loved animals would have given him a puppy.

Once Fred yielded to the temptation of being king of both Sicily and Germany, his twin goals became the conquest of all of Italy, including the Papal States, and, apparently, the substitution of a new religion for Catholicism. He drowned or captured the bishops hastily summoned to a council by Pope Gregory IX to meet the crisis, and mounted an assault on Rome as Pope Gregory was dying. Gregory's successor, Innocent IV, quickly took refuge in France, whence he excommunicated the emperor once again (Fred had already been excommunicated twice before for various offences). Fred died in 1250, but his sons and grandson carried on the struggle for several more years.

Finally, the family — called "the viper's brood" by a pope — was extinguished, and Germany and Italy were left to pick up the pieces. The Kingdom of Sicily would fall to rulers of various nationalities in the centuries to come, while the German kingdom dissolved into its component territories. Later in the thirteenth century, a new Holy Roman emperor emerged from the Hapsburg family, but he did not attempt to unify the area as the earlier German kings had done.

INNOCENT III

The highpoint of medieval papal power and influence is generally considered to be the reign of Innocent III, from 1198 to 1216, and there is much to be said for this view.

He did not aim to control the world, as his enemies have alleged; indeed, some of the texts that have been read that way turn out to have quite other meanings. His energy, intelligence, and forceful personality, combined with his dedication to the rights of the Church, reform, and resistance to heresy and Islam, made his reign one of great achievement. The Fourth Lateran Council; the encouragement of St. Francis, St. Dominic, and other saints; the approval of new orders, including one for the ransom of captives from the Muslims (the Trinitarians, founded by St. John of Matha); the founding of hospitals throughout Europe — these were only some of Innocent's accomplishments. His successors continued his policies, though often with less success due to the German menace.

This great century is so full of larger-than-life personalities and stirring developments that no one chapter and no one book can treat them all. St. Ferdinand of Castile (saintly warrior against the Moors of Spain) and St. Margaret of Hungary (King Bela's daughter and cloistered nun, who was vowed by her father to God if He would remove the scourge of Mongol invasion from Hungary, a living thanksgiving for that deliverance and a sacrifice of reparation for the sins of her people) remind us that Europe was still under siege from more than one direction. St. Elizabeth of Hungary — combining in her twenty-four years of life a romantic and happy marriage, just and merciful rule of Thuringia, motherhood, and a widowhood of penance and charity — embodies the Catholic ideals of her century. St. Gertrude the Great — with her intellectual achievements, widespread influence, and revelations of the Sacred Heart — united the scholarly and mystical lives dear to St. Thomas Aquinas, St. Bonaventure, and other saintly contemporaries.

Had you lived during the thirteenth century, you stood a good chance of actually meeting a saint because there were so many of them and they were so visible. You might even have taken a legal complaint to St. Louis, as he sat under the great oak on his palace grounds, hearing the grievances of the least of his subjects, and dictating his decisions to secretaries. You might have listened, enthralled, to the preaching of Francis, Dominic, or Anthony, or audited one of the courses of St. Thomas Aquinas, as even non-students sometimes did. It seems indeed to have been a blessed time, but it was not to last.

FOOD FOR THOUGHT

If you had to live in the thirteenth century, what country would you prefer? What were some of its advantages and disadvantages? Which of the persons discussed above would you like to know more about and why? Frederick II is one of the most interesting flamboyant villains in history. Do you know of any other figures that might be compared with him?

READING SUGGESTIONS

There are numerous works on the thirteenth century, in addition to those mentioned in the chapter. ***The Glory of Christendom*** (Christendom Press, 1993) — the third volume in Warren Carroll's *A History of Christendom* — covers the general history of the century, as does Henri Daniel-Rops' *Cathedral and Crusade* (E. P. Dutton, 1957). Carroll's book also includes an extensive bibliography on specific topics.

Much has been written on the Albigensian Crusade. Joseph R. Strayer's ***The Albigensian Crusades*** (Dial Press, 1971) is a generally well-written and evenhanded treatment. The edition I have, however, is a reprint that includes a dubious epilogue by a more recent historian devoted to the new historical approach to the study of heresy. The essay criticizes, among other things, "the narrowness of analyzing belief in terms of heresy and orthodoxy." The original edition may be worth getting at the library, but skip the one with the epilogue. ***The Albigensian Crusade***, by Jonathan Sumption (Faber, 1978), is another well-written work that includes useful maps.

Two works on the Mongols, whose invasion of Eastern Europe was another of poor Pope Gregory IX's headaches, may be of interest to some readers. ***The Devil's Horsemen***, by James Chambers (Atheneum, 1979), is a popular account with some interesting sections, particularly those dealing with military affairs. The author does not appear to be a professional historian, and his treatment of the Church and papal policies is somewhat lacking in both understanding and sympathy. A more solid work, though not as broad a history as Chambers', is ***The Mongol Mission***, edited by Christopher Dawson (Sheed and Ward, 1955). This includes actual narratives and letters of Franciscan missionaries in Mongolia and China in the thirteenth and fourteenth centuries; Dawson's introduction is a fine summary of the history of Church-Mongol contacts during this period.

CHAPTER TWELVE

Catholic Thought and Culture in the Thirteenth Century

> *For in his lectures he put out* new *subdivisions, inventing a* new *and clear way of drawing conclusions, and bringing* new *reasons into them....*
> — WILLIAM OF TOCCO, ON ST. THOMAS AQUINAS

How can we discuss, briefly, the civilization of one of the greatest periods in history? How can we summarize the great variety of masterpieces and pioneering work in all areas that characterized the 1200s, or do justice to even one of the great figures? Well, it can't be done. What we can do is sketch a few features of high medieval culture, and mention a few names.

MEDIEVAL ORIGINALITY

It is important to realize that we tend to consider the masterpieces of medieval thought, art, and institutions as comfortable, familiar, and venerable parts of our Catholic heritage. They are reliable precisely because they have been around so long. At the time of their creation, however, what was most striking about them was their originality. Here, again, is William of Tocco gushing about the teaching of St. Thomas Aquinas:

> For in his lectures he put out *new* subdivisions, inventing a *new* and clear way of drawing conclusions, and bringing *new* reasons into them so that no one who had heard him teach *new* doubts and allay them by *new* arguments would have doubted that God had illumined with rays of *new* light one who became straightaway of

such sure judgment that he did not hesitate to teach and write *new* opinions which God had deigned *newly* to inspire.

This was all entirely too new for many of his contemporaries, and both Thomas and his friend St. Bonaventure got into hot water with university and ecclesiastical authorities. We cannot get into that topic, but it is well to recall that novelty was a key feature of medieval achievements.

The newness of Gothic architecture, with its unprecedented technical challenges, must have fascinated architects. (It could also frustrate them, especially when they pushed a spire too high and it fell down.) It was a new thing for whole communities, from lords and ladies, to merchants, to peasant families, to be actually helping to create these sacred masterpieces, all of them wheelbarrowing stone, hauling sand, and setting up columns under the direction of the master builder. How many times in history has the ordinary parishioner been able to look at his church and know, not only that it is beautiful and a real masterpiece, but that he helped build it? (Try not to be bitter about the doughnut-shaped monstrosity with which your parish may be afflicted, and turn your gaze on a book of good photographs of thirteen-century churches. They soothe the soul.)

GOTHIC ARCHITECTURE

My favorite Gothic church is the small jewel box built by St. Louis to house the Crown of Thorns he had brought from Constantinople. Chartres, Notre Dame, and Reims may be more magnificent, but the Sainte Chapelle is something special, and the peculiar thing is that photographs give little idea of its stunning impact.

It is a short walk from Notre Dame in Paris, its spire alone visible above the surrounding medieval and modern government buildings. When you enter it (and it must be a sunny day) you are in a low, gilded and painted small church; it is something of a disappointment after Notre Dame, and you begin to think of lunch. Then you see a small staircase in the corner, up which people are trudging; there is no sign but you follow them. You emerge into a ravishing sea of pure light: it is as if you were, in the words of a contemporary, "introduced into one of heaven's most beautiful rooms." This is the upper church, with the walls seemingly made entirely of light, reflected through over a thousand stained glass panels, most depicting biblical history, with a few devoted to the arrival of the Crown of Thorns in France. It is breathtaking, and unlike many buildings that are exactly like their photographs, this one is totally different. It must be experienced.

MUSIC, LITERATURE, AND POLITICS

The music of the cathedrals was also new: chant was broadening into polyphony, with its new intertwining of voices. Sacred drama — another new thing — was moving out of the church and into the town, where it developed into the tragedies and comedies of later Western theater. Poetry and song in the languages of Europe — rather than in Latin — were also new, and produced masterpieces; Dante was born in the thirteenth century.

Political thought had a striking development in this century; the principles of just government and society were explored by John of Salisbury, St. Thomas, and numerous other writers. The concept of individual rights is generally considered to be an Enlightenment idea, because nobody listens to medievalists. However, as Brian Tierney has shown in his 1997 work, *The Idea of Natural Rights*, the concept is both Christian *and* medieval.

MEDIEVAL SCIENCE

Similarly, science was supposedly born in the seventeenth century with Galileo (actually an indifferent astronomer who was wildly wrong about several things). In fact, as has recently (and grudgingly) been recognized, modern science was born in the Middle Ages. St. Albert the Great, teacher of St. Thomas Aquinas, was the first botanist since ancient times; Roger Bacon pioneered the science of optics. (He may not have invented glasses, as was earlier thought, but somebody else did about the same time, for which I am devoutly grateful.) The study of physics by English scholars evolved in the next century into the field of mathematical physics that anticipated Isaac Newton. Yet we are told over and over again that the time of the Middle Ages was a period of blind superstition when people just couldn't think straight — a neat description of the modern ignoramuses who tell us so.

THE COOLING OF CATHOLIC CHARITY

There is more — so much more — but it is time to investigate what Dom Prosper Guéranger, in his *Liturgical Year* commentary on the institution of the feast of Corpus Christi, alludes to as the "coldness" that made such a feast desirable. He shows how, in more fervent times, the people participated so wholeheartedly and with such faith in the Mass — with all the ceremony and elaborate liturgy with which it was then celebrated — that a separate feast honoring the Sacred Species was not needed. By the middle of the thirteenth century, it was. Why?

Various reasons have been given for the subtle shift in mentality that chilled spirituality. Monsignor Philip Hughes, in his *History of the Church*, seems to fault the papacy for its increasing centralization, involvement in politics, and financial exactions that left the faithful disaffected.

Guéranger sees other reasons for the coldness that was becoming evident in the decline of enthusiastic public and social participation in the Eucharistic sacrifice. The preoccupation of the popes with the German threat may have kept them from pursuing moral reforms more vigorously. Certainly, clerical scandals had not been eliminated, and as Guéranger points out: "The disorders of the sanctuary necessarily brought about relaxation in the people. They grew weary of

> Canon 21: "All the faithful of both sexes shall after they have reached the age of discretion faithfully confess all their sins at least once a year to their own (parish) priest and perform to the best of their ability the penance imposed, receiving reverently at least at Easter the Sacrament of the Eucharist, unless perchance at the advice of their own priest they may for a good reason abstain for a time from its reception; otherwise they shall be cut off from the Church (excommunicated) during life and deprived of Christian burial in death. Wherefore, let this salutary decree be published frequently in the churches, that no one may find in the plea of ignorance a shadow of excuse. But if anyone for a good reason should wish to confess his sins to another priest, let him first seek and obtain permission from his own (parish) priest, since otherwise he (the other priest) cannot loose or bind him.
>
> "Let the priest be discreet and cautious that he may pour wine and oil into the wounds of the one injured after the manner of a skillful physician, carefully inquiring into the circumstances of the sinner and the sin, from the nature of which he may understand what kind of advice to give and what remedy to apply, making use of different experiments to heal the sick one. But let him exercise the greatest precaution that he does not in any degree by word, sign, or any other manner make known the sinner, but should he need more prudent counsel, let him seek it cautiously without any mention of the person. He who dares to reveal a sin confided to him in the tribunal of penance, we decree that he be not only deposed from the sacerdotal office but also relegated to a monastery of strict observance to do penance for the remainder of his life." (Fourth Lateran Council)

receiving the heavenly food from hands that were, but too often, unworthy ones." One indication of lack of devotion to the Holy Eucharist is that the Fourth Lateran Council of 1215 had to oblige the faithful under serious penalties to communicate at least once a year.

HERESY

Another factor in the erosion of Catholic fervor was the growth of heresy. There were many heretical movements during the Middle Ages, but the most formidable and destructive was probably Catharism, mentioned in the previous chapter. It had penetrated the Balkans, Italy, and Austria, before gaining a foothold in southern France.

In its bizarre worldview, harking back to ancient Persian dualism rather than to any form of Christianity, spirit was good, created by God, and matter was evil, created by the devil; therefore marriage and procreation were evil, though it seems sexual perversions were tolerated to some extent. The taking of any kind of oath was forbidden, which meant that no feudal bond, legal commitment, vow, or sworn allegiance to a ruler had any meaning. The goal of your life as a Cathar was to so negate the material part of you that you became one of the "Perfect" — distinguished from the deplorable mass of second-class Cathars who were always trying to eat, drink, and have a good time in spite of how evil those things were. On their deathbeds, these wishy-washy ones would receive the Cathar sacrament, the *Consolamentum,* and promptly depart for the Cathar heaven.

If you were one of the Perfect, however, you took your hatred of matter to such an extreme that you starved yourself to death. Your friends would helpfully keep food from you during your "dissolution," known as the *Endura,* forcibly restraining you if necessary. One of the most horrible aspects of Catharism, described in Emmanuel Le Roy Ladurie's *Montaillou*, was the starvation of infants, who would supposedly, in death, become part of the "Perfect." Cathars were also capable of eliminating their enemies by swifter means, as in the case of at least one papal legate sent to negotiate with them who was murdered on the way.

How to account for the attraction of this creepy cult for so many thirteenth-century Catholics? Here we glimpse a little of the "coldness" that had seeped into the Catholic mind by this time. Particularly in the Languedoc region in southern France, practice had become lax, and fervor declined into tepidity. Priests and religious often led visibly corrupt lives — the Gregorian reforms of the earlier period may not have made it to the easygoing, pleasant-living residents of the warm south. (I can't help thinking of my native California, where life is easy and pleasant, and the cults and mentality are weird beyond belief.)

Even many non-Cathars admired the stern morals of the "Perfect," which contrasted so starkly with Catholic clerical corruption. It is also apparent that the view of matter as evil negated the doctrine of the Holy Eucharist, and may have influenced the decline in Catholic belief and devotion.

The feast of Corpus Christi, devotion to the Sacred Heart, and the great preachers of the new mendicant orders, such as St. Dominic and St. Anthony, did much to combat the apathy of the times, and there is no denying their success. It seems to me, however, that there is yet another reason for the coldness that caused such unease and anxiety among the saints. We will examine it in the following chapters.

FOOD FOR THOUGHT

How would you describe the high culture of our time? What are its greatest achievements in art, architecture, and literature? Are there any dangerous sects around today? Do any of them resemble Catharism in any way?

What has become of the feast of the Sacred Heart and the feast of Corpus Christi, with its public procession of the Blessed Sacrament? Does their status today indicate anything about the fervor of modern Catholics?

READING SUGGESTIONS

Many of the works on the Middle Ages mentioned in earlier chapters are relevant for the thirteenth century also. In addition to them, the biographies of the saints of the century are an almost inexhaustible source of good reading. G. K. Chesterton's little biographies *St. Francis* (1923) and *St. Thomas Aquinas* (1933) are classics (available on the Internet). Another classic is Johannes Jörgensen's more detailed *St. Francis of Assisi: A Biography* (Doubleday, 1955). Mary Purcell's *St. Anthony and His Times* (Hanover House, 1960) is a readable and appealing work; so is *Scholars and Mystics* (H. Regnery Co., 1962), by Sister Mary Jeremy, O.P., on St. Gertrude the Great, her friend St. Mechtild, and other sisters of their convent. Like all Régine Pernoud's works, *Blanche of Castile* (Coward, McCann & Geoghegan, 1975), the life of St. Louis' mother, is both scholarly and readable.

Medieval science and technology have been so slighted in the past that I should mention at least a couple of works on those aspects of medieval life. *Cathedral, Forge, and Waterwheel*, by Frances and Joseph Gies (Harper Collins, 1994), is an interesting survey with some good illustrations. An older work by Lynn White Jr., is *Medieval Technology and Social Change* (Oxford University Press, 1962, 1966). It may be partially outdated but includes stimulating observations; it also sums up rather neatly a discussion of the connection between the increase in grains and legumes in the diet and population and town growth: "In the full sense of the vernacular, the Middle Ages, from the tenth century onward, were full of beans."

CHAPTER THIRTEEN

The Church in the Late Middle Ages

The people of France and of almost the whole world were struck by a blow other than war.

— JEAN DE VENETTE

It might be expected that, if the thirteenth had been such a great century, the following period would build upon it and become as great or greater. Instead, quite the opposite occurred: the fourteenth century was an age of appalling catastrophe, and the fifteenth only slightly less so. During these two centuries — which we can study as one unit, since many things that began in one century culminated in the next — the elements of what I have called "the medieval synthesis" became almost completely unraveled.

THE MEDIEVAL SYNTHESIS AND ITS COLLAPSE

I use the term "medieval synthesis" to refer to a balance or harmony of elements that existed in medieval society. Every civilization includes a number of these elements that coexist within it; it is when they begin to fail or to separate from one another that the civilization begins to weaken and fall. For medieval civilization, it seems to me that five of the key elements were:

- The harmony between Faith and reason.
- The balance of power among nation-states as parts of Christendom.
- The balancing of the authority of the king with local self-government.

- The harmony between the goals of individual self-fulfillment and those of society.
- The equilibrium — often an uneasy one, it is true — between Church and state.

Medieval scholars saw no contradiction between Faith and reason (or between Faith and science, the modern form of the question) because God is the author of all truth, and the source of both human reason and divine Faith. This caused them to be optimistic about the use of reason and the endless possibilities for further study and learning.

Nations might bicker and fight, but the Christian principles of their rulers (with some exceptions, of course), and the astute and professional diplomacy of the Holy See, acting as arbiter of the quarrels within Christendom, maintained the balance among them.

Medieval kings were by no means absolute despots, nor did they wish to be. Their authority was absolute, but their actual exercise of power was limited to what was proper to their office and spelled out in their coronation oaths: usually, the defense of the country and promotion of justice and the general welfare. Local units of society, from parishes to guilds to self-governing towns, ran their own affairs. Authority at the top, in short, and democracy at the bottom; the king took care of the big stuff, and the people took care of their own business.

THE MEDIEVAL INDIVIDUAL

The individual in the Middle Ages has been the subject of interest to some recent historians. How did he see himself or "define" himself? He actually thought little about such questions, of course, being far too busy to think like a modern psychologist. The medieval person existed, not as an isolated individual in a hostile world, as is so often the case today, but within a rich network of *relationships*.

A peasant, for example, was first of all a Catholic; the village church was the center of his life. He was a member of an extended family, to which he had obligations and which had obligations to him. He might be a husband and father, with the rights and duties implicit in those roles. He was a worker with both rights and duties, and access to the local courts if necessary. He stood in a certain customary relationship to the classes above him and those below him. He might be a member of a guild, of either a professional or charitable type. It is within this communitarian context that medieval individuals lived, died, and — if pressed — defined themselves.

CHURCH AND STATE

Finally, there was a balance between Church and state, however rocky the balance might be. Ever since Pope Gelasius I, in a letter to the late-fifth-century Eastern emperor Anastasius, delineated the spheres of both Church and state and explained the relationship between them, the distinction between the two had been acknowledged: "Two there are, august emperor, by which this world is chiefly ruled, the sacred authority of the priesthood and the royal power. Of these the responsibility of the priests is more weighty in so far as they will answer for the kings of men themselves at the divine judgment." (This whole letter — in which the pope spells out the functions and sphere of each authority — is worth reading, and can be found in various collections of early Church documents.)

We have seen that this teaching did not stop rulers from trying to meddle in Church affairs, but in the West this never amounted to the complete domination of either sphere by the other.

FAMINE AND PLAGUE

We can now examine what makes the fourteenth century such a grim period in history — almost a dark age all by itself.

Between 1315 and 1322, another turning point in European history occurred, but this time it was a turn for the

> **From the letter of Pope Gelasius I to Emperor Anastasius:**
>
> You are also aware, dear son, that while you are permitted honorably to rule over human kind, yet in things divine you bow your head humbly before the leaders of the clergy and await from their hands the means of your salvation. In the reception and proper disposition of the heavenly mysteries you recognize that you should be subordinate rather than superior to the religious order, and that in these matters you depend on their judgment rather than wish to force them to follow your will.
>
> "If the ministers of religion, recognizing the supremacy granted you from heaven in matters affecting the public order, obey your laws, lest otherwise they might obstruct the course of secular affairs by irrelevant considerations, with what readiness should you not yield them obedience to whom is assigned the dispensing of the sacred mysteries of religion. Accordingly, just as there is no slight danger in the case of the priests if they refrain from speaking when the service of the divinity requires, so there is no little risk for those who disdain — which God forbid — when they should obey. And if it is fitting that the hearts of the faithful should submit to all priests in general who properly administer divine affairs, how much the more is obedience due to the bishop of that see which the Most High ordained to be above all others, and which is consequently dutifully honored by the devotion of the whole Church."

worse: cold, wet weather ruined crops in northern Europe and the resulting famine produced mass starvation. In some places there was a ten percent mortality rate. Besides this, seven other famines struck southern France during the century; the general agricultural prosperity that underlay the great progress we saw during the High Middle Ages was gone.

As if this were not enough, the middle of the century brought even greater misery. The greatest pandemic in history up to that time, the Black Death, struck Europe. (It seems that only the "Spanish flu" of 1918 was comparable to the Black Death in its effects.) The disease — perhaps originating in the Tatar areas of the Near East — was carried by fleas on infected rats, and arrived in Europe on ships.

It seems to have taken two forms, one less deadly than the other, but both gruesome. The bubonic form caused the distinctive black swellings on the body, among other symptoms, but some victims did survive it. The second form seems to have produced pneumonia or septicemia, and no one survived that; they died so quickly that town authorities were overwhelmed with the number of corpses awaiting burial.

In the two or three years that the Black Death raged through Europe, from about 1347 to 1350, an estimated average of thirty percent of the population of the continent died. In some cases, of course, the death toll was much higher; whole villages might be wiped out. It returned in 1363, and periodically for the next three centuries, causing a population decline that in some places lasted until the eighteenth century. Total deaths for Europe have been put at twenty-five million, with thirteen million for the Middle East and China.

What were the effects on the Church and society? Jean de Venette, a monk who lived through the plague, gives valuable information about a number of points. One distressing feature of life during the plague was the attempt to fix the blame for it on human agents. Lepers were targeted for having supposedly contaminated the wells, and the same charge was leveled against Jews. Local authorities almost everywhere opposed attacks on these victims, but mobs — particularly in Germany — killed numerous Jews, wiping out the entire Jewish population of some German towns.

Another phenomenon associated with the Black Death was the bizarre episode of the Flagellants. These people believed that the plague was a chastisement from God, and therefore they began to do public penance; so far so good, although their public scourgings of themselves must have been gruesome to watch. What got them into trouble, as Venette observes, is that "they began a new sect on their own authority... singing hymns suitable to their rite and newly composed for it." They were not allowed entry into Paris because the theologians "said that this new sect had been formed contrary to the will of God, to the rites of Holy Mother Church, and to the salvation of all their souls." Furthermore, the monk continues, "the Flagellants, supported by certain fatuous priests and monks, were enunciating doctrines and opinions which were beyond measure evil, erroneous, and fallacious. For example, they said that their blood thus drawn by the scourge and poured out was mingled with the blood of Christ. Their many errors showed how little they knew of the Catholic faith." Condemned by Pope Clement VI in 1349, the Flagellants desisted and submitted. Still, this heterodox movement was a sign of headaches to come for the Church.

Another effect of the plague on the Church may have been the lower moral quality of the surviving clergy. Some chroniclers tell us that devoted nuns and priests attended the sick and dying, and they perished, too. The less committed saved their lives by abandoning their sheep and leaving the populated areas until the plague had subsided, when they returned to take up posts vacated by the dedicated (and dead) clergy. How widespread this was is impossible to say, but it probably occurred in at least some parts of Europe.

SOCIAL FRICTION

Another consequence of the Black Death was the rupture in social relations that produced numerous revolts and class antagonism — a sign of the unraveling of communal ties. Venette tells us that following the plague, when the population began to increase,

> the world was not changed for the better but for the worse by this renewal of population. For men were more avaricious and grasping than before, even though they had far greater possessions. They were more covetous and disturbed each other more frequently with suits,

brawls, disputes, and pleas. Nor by the mortality resulting from this terrible plague inflicted by God was peace between kings and lords established. On the contrary, the enemies of the king of France and of the Church were stronger and wickeder than before and stirred up wars on sea and on land.... Although there was an abundance of all goods, yet everything was twice as dear.

The chronicler tells us that there were fewer teachers with the knowledge or willingness to instruct children, so ignorance increased. We find, also, that haunting phrase we came across in the thirteenth century: "Charity," writes the monk, "began to cool, and iniquity with ignorance and sin to abound."

REBELLIONS

The economic dislocation caused by the plague, with its temporary shortage of workers as well as loss of jobs, led in many places to rebellions by the lower classes. Workers thought they should receive higher wages, because there were fewer of them to do necessary work, while their hard-up employers refused.

In England, fourteenth-century chronicler Henry Knighton tells us that after the plague, workers were asking such high wages that crops spoiled because few could afford to pay them. Despite a royal proclamation that workers were not to have more than their customary wages, they continued to demand (and get) much more — an example of the market economy bringing hardship to the countryside. Further measures, from fines to imprisonment, were taken to reduce the "lofty and covetous wishes of the workmen," but their resentment grew and finally broke out into rebellion.

The leaders of the great Peasants' Revolt of 1381 in England actually preached a sort of communism, and appealed to class hostility. At the other end of the economic spectrum, we find the beginnings of mercantile capitalism in the late fourteenth and fifteenth centuries, as banking and moneymaking become all-absorbing activities for businessmen.

THE HUNDRED YEARS' WAR

Ten years before the Black Death struck, the disastrous Hundred Years' War had broken out between England and France. That the two major powers of Europe would battle for over a century was a major disruption in the political balance of Christendom.

France was saved from British conquest by the miracle of St. Joan of Arc. Almost single-handedly, she turned the tide of French defeat into victory and gave her life for it: falling into the hands of the English, she was tried for witchcraft and heresy and burned at the stake. The French king, who owed his crown to her, did not lift a finger to save her then, though he later yielded to the entreaties of Joan's mother for a process of rehabilitation. As for the English, no sooner had they gone home following their defeat in 1453 than they fell into a destructive civil war for the throne of England, which continued for most of the following three decades.

TURKISH ATTACKS

Further disasters loomed for Europe in these centuries. In 1354, the Ottoman Turks, recent arrivals from central Asia and converts to Islam who were busy conquering what remained of the tottering Byzantine Empire, crossed from Asia into Europe. At the time, only their victims in the Balkans and Greece seem to have paid much attention. However, when — ninety-nine years later — they conquered the supposedly impregnable Constantinople, all of Europe trembled. It was the beginning of the great onslaught of Islam upon Europe that has, perhaps, never ended.

THE PAPACY IN DISTRESS

There's more. From the start of the period, the papacy was in trouble. The insult to Pope Boniface VIII at Anagni in 1303, a confused melee in which both a French delegation and Italian enemies of the pope seemed to have played a role, represents a breakdown in Church-state relations. The issue was a political, not a doctrinal, one (taxation of French clergy in certain circumstances), but the aged pontiff was badly shaken up by the incident and died not long after returning to Rome.

Following the seven-month pontificate of Benedict XI, many of the cardinals thought it wise to elect someone more acceptable to the French King Philip IV; their choice in 1305, Clement V, was so acceptable that he never left France. Instead, he set up the papal court in Avignon, which was technically not on French soil at the time but was certainly within the French sphere.

To be fair, there were reasons in favor of his choice. Avignon was nearer to the center of Europe, farther from Muslim attacks by sea, healthier in climate, and not full of those turbulent Italians who so often interfered with even the best of popes. Still, Peter had left Rome — not just to take up residence in another Italian city, as had happened in the past, but for another country — and Christendom was scandalized. It was not until 1377 that this "Babylonian Captivity" of the Avignon Papacy ended, through the efforts of many earnest Catholics including the charismatic and persistent St. Catherine of Siena, and the pope returned to Rome.

Did that solve the Church's problems? It should have, but instead they became a thousand times worse. The papal election of 1378 produced a stern reformer, so harsh that some of the cardinals decided they had made a mistake and began to claim they had been pressured by the Roman mob during the election. They proceeded to another election, so there were now two claimants to the papal throne. For the three decades of this Great Schism of the West there were two — sometimes three — claimants to the papal office, and almost no one in Europe could figure out who was the real one. There were saints on both sides of the issue, and meanwhile the Church drifted this way and that. At the Council of Constance (1414-1417) the matter was settled, and there was once again one pope, reigning in Rome.

Was this the end of the Church's troubles? Not by a long shot. Now it was some members of the Council who began to say that, since it was they who had settled the schism, councils — not the popes — must be the highest authority in the Church. This is the heresy of Conciliarism, finally condemned in 1460.

How far these grave troubles were responsible for the quality of the Renaissance popes is debatable. It is true, however, that during the late fifteenth century and into the next, we find the popes acting more like Italian Renaissance princes than pastors of the universal Church.

POSITIVE DEVELOPMENTS

Is there any more bad news from the Late Middle Ages? Unfortunately, yes, and it will be discussed in the next chapter. The Renaissance will be there, too — a phenomenon that is both good and bad news.

Is there any good news? There is, from fifteenth-century Spain. In 1469, the young heiress of Castile married the young heir of Aragon, and the famous royal team of Ferdinand and Isabella was formed. They proceeded to unify the many kingdoms of the Iberian Peninsula, most of which had by now fought their way out of Moorish domination, and reform both government and Church in Spain. They also completed the *Reconquista* of the peninsula by driving the Moors from their last stronghold of Granada in 1492.

During the siege (at which Isabella was present, though she was pregnant at the time), a mariner turned up with a scheme of sailing west to reopen the European trade routes with Asia that had been cut off by the Ottoman Turks. This sailor — Christopher Columbus, of course — had already been turned down by several potential sponsors, but Isabella saw the merit of his project. She financed the outfitting of three ships; following the fall of Granada to the Spaniards, the little fleet sailed out to brave the Atlantic and to discover the great and unexpected geographical obstacle in the way of quick trips to China. The advantages of American colonies for Spain, and the number of souls in the Americas to be gained for Christ, remained largely unknown until the following century, which would begin the golden age of Spain.

FOOD FOR THOUGHT

Is there a "modern synthesis," comparable to the medieval synthesis, holding our society together? What are some of its commonly accepted principles? Do any of them show signs of weakening at this time?

We have had nothing comparable to the Black Death since the early twentieth century. Is there any danger of a similar pandemic occurring today, or is modern science able to prevent such outbreaks?

The Ottoman threat to Europe increased spectacularly during the Late Middle Ages, although the Muslims were driven from Spain by the end of the period. How does the balance sheet look today? Is there still a Muslim threat to Europe, and in what particular areas? Think of concrete examples.

READING SUGGESTIONS

There are many works available on this period, and some fine biographies of its main personalities. The multivolume histories of the Church cited in previous chapters are useful here for looking up specific events, as are detailed histories of the papacy such as Ludwig von Pastor's *History of the Popes* (Herder, publishing dates vary). There are a number of books about the Black Death, but they are so detailed that I find I'm being told more than I care to know about it.

The Hundred Years' War, by Edouard Perroy, a French historian, is a good summary of that period; a paperback edition of the English translation was published by Capricorn Books in 1965.

A very worthwhile work, quite brief, is *The Later Middle Ages* (Hawthorn Books, Inc., 1960), by Bernard Guillemain.

This is a volume in the *Twentieth Century Encyclopedia of Catholicism*, edited by Henri Daniel-Rops, and bears an *Imprimatur* and *Nihil Obstat*. It deals with the period from the thirteenth to the mid-fifteenth century, and unfortunately lacks an index. Topics are easy to locate, however, in such a short book.

One of the best books on St. Joan of Arc seems to me to be Hilaire Belloc's very short work, *Joan of Arc*, written in the literary style of a simple chronicle of the period but obviously based on the primary sources, which has been reprinted by The Neumann Press. I believe Régine Pernoud has written more than one work on St. Joan. A particularly interesting one is **Joan of Arc: By Herself and Her Witnesses** (Scarborough House, 1994).

(I have one caveat concerning the biographies of Joan that I have read, which is that they all seem to admit that she did sign a confession, though she retracted it later. A recent French scholar has made an excellent case for the view that she did not sign the document, and future works on the saint may take this into account.)

William Thomas Walsh's **Isabella of Spain: The Last Crusader (1451-1504)** is a massive older work (original 1930 edition reprinted by Tan Books and Publishers, 1987). Warren Carroll's **Isabel of Spain: The Catholic Queen** (Christendom Press, 1991) is a fine biography that utilizes Walsh's work while also making use of more recent material and drawing on primary sources.

CHAPTER FOURTEEN

Catholic Thought and Culture in the Late Middle Ages

"The end justifies the means."
— NICCOLÒ MACHIAVELLI

As with the political and social developments of this shaky period, the news from the cultural front is nearly all bad. In the 1300s, we find serious and long-lasting heresies emerging, as well as a new and disastrous philosophical approach.

To take the heresies first, we find the Englishman John Wycliffe studying at Oxford and becoming a priest in the mid-fourteenth century. He attracted attention and praise for his sermons and lectures attacking the temporal possessions and power of the Church, and calling for a return to apostolic poverty. So far he was criticizing disorders that others had also; he did not stop there, however.

Soon he proceeded to attack almost all essential points of Catholic doctrine, in a sort of eerie foreshadowing of the teachings of the later Protestant revolutionaries. Transubstantiation, the divine origin of the hierarchy, confession, Holy Orders, indulgences, and many other Catholic doctrines and practices met with his stern rejection. Like Martin Luther, he preached *sola scriptura* — "Scripture alone," minus Tradition — as the rule of faith. Like Calvin, he preached predestination. Again, as in the case of Luther and the German peasants, country people accepted some of Wycliffe's ideas and put them into practice in the Peasants' Revolt of 1381.

The following year, both the English Church and the royal court realized what they were dealing with in the person of Wycliffe, and he was condemned and fired from his Oxford teaching position. His death two years later did not, unfortunately, also mean the death of his heretical notions.

JOHN HUS

Oddly enough, Bohemia, in Eastern Europe, had considerable contact with England at this time, due to the academic contacts that followed the marriage of King Richard II to the daughter of Bohemia's king. John Hus was a professor at the University of Prague who came to hear of Wycliffe's theories and embrace most of them, though he had his own new ideas, too. He did not reject Transubstantiation, for example, but he insisted on Communion under both Species. He also inveighed against real abuses within the Church, and gained a considerable following.

Investigated, condemned, and excommunicated, Hus continued to stir up the Czechs of Bohemia and deny the authority and jurisdiction of the popes. Holy Roman Emperor Sigismund had summoned Hus to appear before the Council of Constance, and Hus seemed willing to use the opportunity to explain his beliefs to the assembly. He was examined and then imprisoned in a monastery for some months until the Council could get around to putting him on trial formally. (The Council members had the more pressing business of settling the Great Schism first.)

When the process finally began in June 1415, Hus answered evasively and argued over the meanings of words such as "abjure," which he was of course asked to do with respect to his heresies, and which he refused to do. In a last-ditch attempt to avoid condemning him to death for heresy, a conciliatory formula was presented to him to sign, and he refused that, too. Hus was turned over to the secular authority, the duke of Bavaria, who also attempted to persuade him to renounce his errors. All efforts having failed, he was burned at the stake on July 6, 1415. Opposition to the Church's refusal of the Precious Blood to the laity became a hallmark of followers of Hus in Bohemia for centuries; it was also the rallying point of their rebellions and wars in the following decades.

NOMINALISM

Bad as these heresies were, it might be argued that a fourteenth-century Franciscan, William of Ockham, did far more damage to the Western mind with his new ideas in philosophy and theology.

We have seen something of the thought of St. Thomas Aquinas, and how it reflected the *realism* that characterized Aristotle and the classical mind in general. St. Thomas was careful to distinguish the areas in which the mind can arrive at truth through reason alone from those in which it requires faith, and he had great confidence in the use of reason. He also held, with Aristotle, that the human mind is capable of attaining universal concepts. (For example, if we make the acquaintance of a dog, our intellects abstract from sense data the essence of the creature — a universal idea that can be applied to all other dogs in the world, no matter what their size or appearance. When we go to a dog show, our minds recognize that all the animals we see are, underneath the fuzz, included in that universal concept we call "dog." Similarly, we use the word "man" — *pace* the feminists — to express the essence shared by all human beings.)

This seems obvious to anyone who has thought it through, but Ockham denied it. He said the mind does not get at universal concepts or the real essence of things (what makes a thing to be what it is, such as "dogness" existing in all dogs); all we experience are individual things, to which we sometimes give the same names (*nomina*) merely for the sake of convenience. We cannot really arrive at any general meaning, coherence, or conclusion from this experience. Ockham seems to deny the reality of what is known by the intellect, and implicitly to claim that only what is perceived by the senses is real. He also denied that God can be known through nature, as Christians from St. Paul to St. Thomas had held.

This is the beginning of pessimism or skepticism in philosophy — a lack of confidence in the ability of the mind to know truth, in opposition to the confidence of Thomas in the mind's capacity. In this it foreshadows the whole subsequent development (or decline) of Western thought. Ockham seems also to have held that something can be true and false at the same time — true for faith and false for reason, and vice versa; that sin and grace can coexist in the same person, but that sin is sort of covered up by grace — an idea generally associated with Luther, who was very possibly influenced by Ockham's thought.

EFFECTS OF NOMINALISM ON THEOLOGY

The consequences of Nominalism for theology were far-reaching, and Robert A. Sungenis, in his 1997 book *Not By Scripture Alone*, has analyzed some of them.

The idea that reality is not what is perceived by the intellect, but the "changing, individual, empirical facts" perceived by the senses, affects how one views the sacraments. It leads to skepticism about the connection between earthly and heavenly things, so that sacraments are seen as only symbolic, Christ is only "nominally" in the Holy Eucharist, justification is merely "nominal," and so on. Sungenis sees this attitude as foreshadowing the preoccupation of modern philosophers with language rather than with reality. He quotes Louis Dupré in *Passage to Modernity* as saying that "the effect of nominalist theology was to remove God from creation so that nature came to be seen as linked only externally to God. The burden of interpreting nature and constituting meaning then fell to the human self."

This subjectivism is another feature of late medieval culture, as we will see shortly. Ockham's thought is difficult, and there is much more to it than I have tried to explain here. I don't pretend to understand all of it. I think we can see, though, that he was bad news.

THE RENAISSANCE

"All right, all right," you may be thinking, "but wasn't there a really good thing going on at this time called the Renaissance?" Well, yes — in a way. The Renaissance had started in the fourteenth century and was roaring into high gear by the fifteenth. It is time to take a look at it.

The Renaissance may be considered as a period of cultural development, particularly in the visual arts, which began around 1350 in Italy. In his biography of St. Thomas Aquinas, G. K. Chesterton says that the Renaissance "was a resurrection of old things discovered in a dead thing [the ancient world]," in contrast to the "great growth of new things produced by a living thing," which was medieval culture. In the arts, the Renaissance was not a "new beginning" or even "rebirth," because art wasn't dead in the first place. It may be seen as a revival in the limited sense that it occurred after the devastation of the Black Death, but Giotto, the first artist who learned to use perspective (a Renaissance hallmark), died before the plague.

What intellectuals of the time, who were nearly all Italian Catholics, thought were being "reborn" were classical Latin and Greek. Petrarch, for example, wanted to write like Cicero, in "pure" Latin rather than in the scholarly medieval Latin then in use. (I have read that Petrarch's writings in what he took to be classical Latin style are unreadable — unlike his graceful Italian works.)

The "rebirth" was, in other words, originally a linguistic revival. But classical languages are inseparable from classical texts, and the ideas and mentality expressed in the texts began to fascinate some scholars (and artists) more than the languages themselves. It was not that the texts were new; for the most part, what Renaissance scholars studied were not lost masterpieces they had unearthed but books preserved in monasteries for centuries and used by medieval scholars and in schools. The way in which medieval students approached ancient writings, however, differed from that of their later counterparts. Their viewpoint was thoroughly Catholic, and they recognized the moral and philosophical flaws in what they read, while also acknowledging the good they found. Later Renaissance intellectuals breathed a different cultural air. They let themselves be fascinated by the pagan ideas they found in the ancient classics, and adopted the worldly outlook of the authors they studied. We will see shortly where this led.

THE FINE ARTS

Meanwhile, it seems true to say that the most spectacular progress during the Renaissance was in art, and particularly in painting. Once artists were able to use perspective to make their pictures more lifelike — something they had long strived to do — great advances could be made in technique. From Giotto's frescoes in Padua and Assisi to Michelangelo's spectacular ceiling, Renaissance art is ravishing. Notice, however, that its themes change from the early to the later Renaissance. Early art draws largely on Christian or biblical themes; it is somewhat later that we get the goddesses rising from the sea and other scenes of the old pagan deities. (I am not saying that they are poor art, but that they represent a different approach from that of earlier artists.)

RENAISSANCE THOUGHT: PICO

Sculpture, architecture, and the minor arts also flourished (though Chesterton called the Renaissance in architecture "the Relapse"), in which a similar progression from Christian to pagan themes is observable. Still, though there was much continuity in the arts with the medieval period, there were some developments in other areas during the Renaissance that really were new in the history of Christendom. One of these was the glorification of man.

Some Renaissance artists and writers, interested in reviving themes they found in ancient pagan texts, went further than any ancient writer in glorifying the human individual. A prime example of this trend is Pico della Mirandola's *Oration on the Dignity of Man*. In this work, Pico depicts God telling Adam that his nature has no limits, and that he may in effect create himself.

This is a new idea in history, with many consequences. I cannot imagine any Hebrew, Greek, Roman, or medieval thinker who would have written such a thing. Even the ancient pagans generally had an awe of their gods and a concept of the limitations of human nature, as well as of the dangers of pride (hubris) that precluded such an extravagant exaltation of themselves. Not so the pagans of the Renaissance.

> **From *Oration on the Dignity of Man*, by Pico della Mirandola:**
>
> At last, the Supreme Maker decreed that this creature, to whom He could give nothing wholly his own, should have a share in the particular endowment of every other creature. Taking man, therefore, this creature of indeterminate image, He set him in the middle of the world and thus spoke to him:
>
> "'We have given you, O Adam, no visage proper to yourself, nor endowment properly your own, in order that whatever place, whatever form, whatever gifts you may, with premeditation, select, these same you may have and possess through your own judgment and decision. The nature of all other creatures is defined and restricted within laws which We have laid down; you, by contrast, impeded by no such restrictions, may, by your own free will, to whose custody We have assigned you, trace for yourself the lineaments of your own nature. I have placed you at the very center of the world, so that from that vantage point you may with greater ease glance round about you on all that the world contains. We have made you a creature neither of heaven nor of earth, neither mortal nor immortal, in order that you may, as the free and proud shaper of your own being, fashion yourself in the
>
> *(continued on page 152)*

> (continued from page 151)
>
> form you may prefer. It will be in your power to descend to the lower, brutish forms of life; you will be able, through your own decision, to rise again to the superior orders whose life is divine.'
>
> "Oh unsurpassed generosity of God the Father, Oh wondrous and unsurpassable felicity of man, to whom it is granted to have what he chooses, to be what he wills to be! The brutes, from the moment of their birth, bring with them, as Lucilius says, 'from their mother's womb' all that they will ever possess. The highest spiritual beings were, from the very moment of creation, or soon thereafter, fixed in the mode of being which would be theirs through measureless eternities. But upon man, at the moment of his creation, God bestowed seeds pregnant with all possibilities, the germs of every form of life. Whichever of these a man shall cultivate, the same will mature and bear fruit in him. If vegetative, he will become a plant; if sensual, he will become brutish; if rational, he will reveal himself a heavenly being; if intellectual, he will be an angel and the son of God. And if, dissatisfied with the lot of all creatures, he should recollect himself into the center of his own unity, he will there become one spirit with God, in the solitary darkness of the Father, Who is set above all things, himself transcend all creatures."

RENAISSANCE THOUGHT: MACHIAVELLI

"Man can do all things if only he will" was another Renaissance slogan. The glorification of the powerful individual and his sovereignty would reach a certain climax in Niccolò Machiavelli's *The Prince*. This famous, and infamous, political treatise advises rulers to ignore Christian morality, and implicitly rejects both the divine origin of political authority and the ruler's obligation to govern in accord with Christian principles. In one famous statement, Machiavelli sets forth a principle of political action that no previous writer — whether Hebrew, Greek, Roman, or Christian — would have accepted; it would, however, be admired and acted upon by all modern tyrants, and by lesser political figures everywhere: "... in the actions of men, and especially of princes, from which there is no appeal, the end justifies the means."

We are so used to hearing this that perhaps we are not startled by it until we think it out. The notion, however, that once we have a goal in view we can do anything in order to attain it is not only unprecedented in Western politics, it is... well... Machiavellian.

The Renaissance, then, is a mixed bag. It is full of beauty dedicated to the glory of God, but also of insidious emphases and ideas that will embed themselves in the Western mind.

There remains one last feature of this epoch that we need to consider, one which may shed the most light on the meaning of those puzzling references to "coldness" in perhaps the most Catholic of all centuries, the thirteenth — and which, in turn, has affected the fourteenth, fifteenth, and all subsequent centuries up to our time. This is the growth of secularism, which can be described as a preoccupation with the things of this world, specifically the emphasis on moneymaking that came with the new proto-capitalist enterprises and business methods that developed during the Late Middle Ages. This represents a shift from the medieval mentality that centered all life's activities around the goal of loving union with God and acting on Christian principles. Christianity was certainly not incompatible with economic progress, as we have seen in the earlier medieval period, but the new attitude tended to put religion and spiritual concerns in a compartment (the Sunday compartment) separate from the rest of life.

THE RISE OF BUSINESS CULTURE

The Greeks had defined man as a rational animal, whose life was not ordered to mere sense gratification. By the nineteenth century, man was being defined as "an acquisitive animal," with the emphasis on economic activity. In between, the ages of Faith defined man and his end in terms of Christian principles. In practice, however, this definition was being watered down as early as the thirteenth century. The growth of banking and other business activities, combined with a more individualist outlook, began to compete with communitarian guild principles.

Our Lord had said, "You cannot serve God and mammon [money]," but late medieval merchants gave it a good try. In the eighteenth century, Franz Josef Haydn, a Catholic composer, headed every sheet of his music with "*Ad majorem dei gloriam*" ("To the greater glory of God"). In the fifteenth century, however, an Italian merchant was heading each page of his ledger with "In the name of God and Profit."

A French medievalist, Georges Duby, in *The Knight, the Lady, and the Priest: The Making of Modern Marriage in Medieval France*, writes that the early medieval people he studied did not think primarily in economic terms. They could be greedy, for power and other things, but it was only in the thirteenth century that this was slowly becoming transformed into *avaritia* — the desire for money. (St. Francis of Assisi would have seen this firsthand, since his father was a prosperous cloth merchant.)

There is no question that business and moneymaking had begun to loom larger in medieval life, and it seems to me that this focus, reinforced by the Renaissance cult of individual success, was at least one source of the "coldness" that had begun to seep into Catholic life. The businessman is interested in making and keeping money, not in giving it away to the unproductive poor. Time is money, too, and he does not care to spend too much of that in church or following Corpus Christi processions.

One historian has summed up this shift in focus from the spiritual to the worldly by saying that in their souls many Catholics began to keep two sets of books: one for themselves, and one for God. Gone, though not entirely, was the wholeness of an earlier Christendom, in which the Faith had permeated every aspect of life. Now it found itself in a separate, sometimes rarely opened, Sunday book.

This is a melancholy close to the age that was so full of Catholic glory, and the age that will follow is in some ways even more depressing, as many of the ideas discussed in this chapter work themselves out to their logical conclusions. Nevertheless, God will still be with His people, and the number of saints He will raise up in the sixteenth and seventeenth centuries will rival that of the twelfth and thirteenth. They were desperately needed, as we shall see, perhaps, in a future volume.

FOOD FOR THOUGHT

Are there really people today who think like Machiavelli? (Resist the temptation to say, "All politicians." Try to think of specific examples of how his principles have — or have not — been applied.)

What do you think of the possible connection between moneymaking and lack of religious fervor? There are usually multiple causes of historical developments. Can you think of any other explanation for why charity was "growing cold," in the eyes of St. Francis and other Churchmen, as early as the 1200s? Where is the love of God and neighbor most evident today, in your experience?

READING SUGGESTIONS

James J. Walsh, author of *The Thirteenth, Greatest of Centuries* (eleventh edition published by Fordham University Press, 1943), also wrote *The Century of Columbus* (Catholic Summer School Press, 1914), which treats of the period from 1450 to 1550. The work thus goes beyond our time frame for the Late Middle Ages, and includes the early Reformation. I cannot pretend to share his upbeat assessment of the period, but much of what he discusses in the book is of interest. Since Walsh was a medical doctor, the sections on hospitals and medical care in the late medieval period are very worthwhile; also worth reading are his discussions of the guilds, then still functioning on their original Catholic principles. The sections on Renaissance art are good, but suffer (at least in my edition) from lack of illustrations. He writes of Pico's piety and St. Thomas More's admiration of him, but there is no discussion of the *Oration on the Dignity of Man*. He also writes very positively about Machiavelli (who really did some good historical work), but does not comment on the statement in *The Prince* that I have criticized above. We also do not learn from Walsh that some of the works of both of these authors were censured by the Church.

There are many studies of the thought of William of Ockham, but I have not included them here because of their technical complexity and limited appeal for the general reader.

Renaissance art must be seen to be appreciated; if you are fortunate enough to live near a good museum, visit its Renaissance collection and notice the differences in style and themes between early and late Renaissance pictures. There are also many fine books on Renaissance art, lavishly illustrated. I am fond of Bernard Berenson's **The Italian Painters of the Renaissance** (published in various editions, including one by Meridian, 1968). The author was not a Catholic when he wrote this major study — though he became one later on — but he has an obvious sympathy with and enthusiasm for the religious art of the time as well as for its secular works. His theory of how our minds respond to art — developed in **Aesthetics and History** (published in various editions, including one by Doubleday, 1965) — is out of favor now. The reason? Possibly because it provided an objective basis for judging and appreciating art, while modern thought is subjectively based — but it makes great sense to me. For those interested in art and art history, it is a fascinating little book.

APPENDIX A

Making Sense of It All

We have just been galloping through a thousand years of history, and it may seem to you that we encountered — fleetingly — a great many dates, people, events, and developments. Those mentioned in the chapters, however, represent a tiny fraction of the historical data for the periods we visited. If you wanted to know more, where would you start?

This is not the place for a course, or even a lecture, on historiography, but the following suggestions may be helpful to those who would like to undertake a systematic study of Catholic history.

1. THERE IS NO SUBSTITUTE FOR CHRONOLOGY

I emphasize this because there has been a tendency in recent history teaching to downplay or even eliminate dates. In part this was a reaction to an earlier emphasis on memorization of dates and events that sometimes slighted the broader picture — as if "In fourteen hundred ninety-two Columbus sailed the ocean blue" told the whole story. The result of ignoring dates, however, is that our students often have no idea of whether Charlemagne came before or after Columbus.

Dates are the bones of history: just as you can't have a body without a skeleton, you can't have a coherent view of the past without the framework of events and when they happened.

There are several ways of organizing chronology, and browsing various history textbooks — preferably older ones — will give you some ideas for constructing time lines. You may decide to group the historical information you want to retain in outline form, with Roman and Arabic numerals alternating with capital and lowercase letters as the framework for a period of time. For the Roman Christian period, the beginning of your chronology might look like this:

I. Early Roman Empire, 27 B.C. – A.D. 180
    A. Augustus Caesar — 27 B.C. – A.D. 14
        1. Pax Romana
        2. beginning of Christianity
            (a) census of the empire, 1 B.C.
            (b) birth of Our Lord, December, 1 B.C.
    B. Tiberius — 14-37
        1. preaching of John the Baptist
        2. Crucifixion and Ascension of Our Lord, c. 30
    C. Nero — 54-68
        1. fire in Rome, 64
        2. first persecution of the Christians; death of St. Peter, 64

This is merely an illustration of the outline form. In practice, more material would have to be included, but you get the idea. (On the census and Our Lord's birth, by the way, the most recent historical and archaeological studies support the traditional dates.) With a detailed outline, you are grouping the most important dates and events so that you can read down the page and get a snapshot of a given time period.

Another method, more suitable for later periods, is making a chart that shows dates in a column in the left and, in ruled columns for each major country or area, what was going on at that time. Thus, the page — or large index card — for the eleventh century would include, on the left, the years 1000, 1054 (Catholic-Orthodox schism), 1066 (Norman Conquest), 1077 (Emperor Henry IV submits to the pope at Canossa), and 1096 (First Crusade). The other columns would show what was going on in England, France, Germany, the papacy, and the Eastern Empire at approximately those times. The Norman Conquest, for example, would appear in both the English and French columns, with a few explanatory notes; the eleventh-century economic revival might be noted across the top of the chart opposite the year 1000; the names of some of the main rulers could be noted in the country columns; a "culture" column could be added at the far right. The advantage of this method is that it allows one to see what is going on at the same time all over the area one is studying. This is important because too often we lose sight of the broad picture when we focus on one event in one area.

It is also possible to organize historical material by theme. The topic of the Church in the Roman Empire might include sections, of a few sentences each, dealing with origins, organization, the papacy, Roman attitudes and persecutions, and so on. Dates and specific events and persons would also, of course, appear in this format.

The tedious truth is that mastering history involves organizing it in all these ways. You might start with a chronology. But the more you learn, the more you will need to spread it out in a chart, and the more you will need to make notes of intricate controversies or complex events.

2. THE FOUR WAYS TO COMMIT INFORMATION TO MEMORY

If you are going to give time and effort to a serious study of history, presumably you would like to remember what you learn. The ways of putting data into our memory banks are: reading, writing, hearing, and speaking.

Reading about a historical event is one way of remembering it. However, as anyone knows who has read a detailed account of a war, for example, it is not enough to fix the information clearly in our minds. This is why we take notes and make time lines — in other words, we *write out* what we want to remember. The process of writing is another way of storing information in our brains.

What about hearing? For students, this is the way they learn from lectures — or are supposed to learn — but notice that they are also expected to take notes in order to retain the material presented. (Sadly, few students now have the skills to take lecture notes, and the results are apparent in their grades.) If you are not attending history lectures, you can still learn history. But it can also be a good thing, at least occasionally, to borrow some good history videos from the library or listen to a recorded lecture on something you are working on.

Speaking, the fourth way of putting information into the memory, is easy for teachers who get to recite what they have learned (indeed, they know it so well that they can babble it in their sleep), but not so easy for others. Students preparing for exams often put key information on file cards (writing, again) and get someone to ask them questions from the cards. Absent a willing accomplice, the student can recount the course of the Hundred Years' War to a dog, cat, parrot (who might learn to say, "Agincourt!"), or simply to the mirror. The point, however silly it may sound, is that reciting helps solidify your recollections of data you have already read, written, and heard. Friends who share a serious interest in history have an advantage, because discussing and arguing combine the modes of hearing and speaking.

3. ASK WHAT, WHEN, WHY, SO WHAT?

These are the key questions to ask about anything in history. If you can answer these questions about any historical happening, you have understood it, at least at a basic level. The question "What?" requires a definition: What, precisely, are we talking about? What is the essence of the heresy in question, what are the most important points about Emperor So-and-So, what is meant by the investiture controversy?

We also need to know the answer to "When?" for any historical happening, and often "Where?" will be just as important: events must be situated in space and time.

The two final questions are the most important because they deal with causality and consequences. "Why?" will often involve multiple causes, and you will need to sort them out and focus on the most important. "So what?" requires two levels of response: results (both immediate and long-term) and the historical significance of the event (why we study it).

For example, one immediate result of the seventeenth-century Thirty Years' War was the devastation and depopulation of some of the German states, and the radical weakening of the Holy Roman Empire. Long-term consequences include the rise of France to the position of top European power. The significance of this war for historians can include a number of points. One that interests me is how this war was almost a dress rehearsal for World War I: it began as a local conflict that escalated into the first general European war in modern history. How the escalation occurred is both interesting and instructive.

It is worth pointing out here that the ancients saw history as part of ethics; one learned about morality by observing how people of the past behaved. For Catholics, history is more than that: it is God's working in the world. Our "So what?" will therefore always be open to seeing God's hand in everything that happens in history. In some cases, His guidance will be easy to discern, while in others we may not see it at all. It is always, nevertheless, at work in the human affairs we study.

4. FIND YOUR SPECIAL INTEREST

After gaining an overview of Church history, you will generally find that you are drawn to some particular area, theme, or person. Investigating this interest systematically is one of the most rewarding facets of historical study. Instead of merely superficial general knowledge, you arrive at a comprehensive understanding of one short period, one war, one pontificate, one heresy, one saint.

No matter how limited the topic, you will probably find a large number of books and articles dealing with it, and sifting through them can be both a pleasure and a valuable learning experience — it is detective work, in fact. Soon you come to know enough to evaluate the strengths and weaknesses of your sources, and perhaps even spot an unexplored area in which you might like to do primary research someday. The knowledge thus gained is a satisfaction in itself, but it may also lead you on to further exploration. Before you know it, you may actually be . . . a historian!

APPENDIX B

Evaluating History Books

Where does the reader begin, if he wants to explore Catholic history beyond the reading suggestions for each chapter? I have avoided drawing up a comprehensive bibliography for three reasons.

In the first place, merely listing the hundreds of works pertaining to the period covered in this volume would not seem to be of much help to the general reader who only wants the titles of a few good books on specific topics. In the second place, bibliographies are soon outdated, sometimes before they have got into print. In the third place, non-Catholic, or even anti-Catholic, works that the specialist can profitably use because he can sort out the wheat from the chaff are not suitable for the general reader without qualifications that would overextend the bibliography pages.

What I am doing here instead is giving general guidelines for evaluating history books you come across, and a method for pursuing topics that interest you.

First, evaluation. You come across a book in a bookstore or in the library on what looks like Catholic history. How do you know it is worth reading, or whether it will mislead you on some important point? The *Imprimatur* and *Nihil Obstat* are good indicators of doctrinally sound material, but they do not routinely appear on works of history, even by Catholic historians. The Church histories of Henri Daniel-Rops and Monsignor Philip Hughes carry them, but works by Christopher Dawson and Henri Marrou do not, nor do Warren Carroll's more recent *History of Christendom* volumes. This does not mean in any way that the latter works are not reliable, but that the requirements for ecclesiastical approval have changed in recent decades, and in any case they tended to apply more to clerical than to lay authors. Still, official approbation is a good sign if one is examining an older work.

Look for some indication that the author is Catholic, since a Catholic writer will obviously have more sympathy for his subject. (This does not necessarily apply to contemporary Catholic historians, some of whom have adopted a secularist mentality that diminishes their work.) There are, of course, non-Catholic writers such as Eleanor Shipley Duckett, Henry Osborn Taylor, Amy Kelly and other medievalists of the first half of the twentieth century whose works are both first-rate and unbiased, so we need not make it a rule to read only Catholic historians.

If you are looking for a truly scholarly work, make sure the author cites primary sources; these are the raw material of history, and all secondary works draw upon them. A historian will use secondary sources as well, but he should show the reader that he has utilized at least some of the basic works written during the period he is discussing. He should also show a grasp of the secondary literature in more than one language. A book written in English that only cites other books written in English — no primary sources, no foreign-language works — is often not worth much. You might as well just read the other books the author used. As with all rules, there are exceptions to this one. Most of the notes in the original French works by some excellent historians, such as Daniel-Rops, have been omitted in the English translations, though the books are still worth reading.

The author should have academic credentials. Medieval history especially has suffered from non-specialists who somehow think they should write books about what they do not know.

An example is William Manchester's *A World Lit Only By Fire — The Medieval Mind and the Renaissance: Portrait of an Age*, deservedly excoriated by Professor Norman Cantor of Columbia University in a *Washington Post* book review. This critique by a Jewish medievalist illustrates the objectivity that characterizes good history; Cantor refers to Dom David Knowles as a "great medievalist" in a neat passage. After observing that Manchester takes a very dim view of the Middle Ages, claiming that the period had a low level of culture and technology and was inferior to Rome, Cantor remarks: "Although the great medievalists David Knowles and Richard Southern are listed in Manchester's bibliography, he apparently doesn't believe a word they ever wrote on the astonishingly high degree of cultural creativity in the Middle Ages, certainly the equal of Roman achievement." Cantor quotes Manchester as writing that "Catholicism . . . found its greatest strength in total resistance to change," and Cantor explains how, on the contrary, "the Church was often in the vanguard of change."

Cantor also points to what he calls "a distressing revival of the worst kind of 19th-century anti-Catholicism" in the book under review, and repeats in closing that "it is distressing to think that this anti-Christian diatribe, reviving the wildest and most ignorant 19th-century polemics against the Catholic Church, will with the publisher's heavy promotion make its way into thousands of middle-class households and school libraries." I know. It made its way into my Catholic doctor's library, and I had to spend a good part of a medical appointment last year explaining that it is tripe.

As a minimum, then, check out the academic background of the author in whom you are interested. He may not be a historian at all, or he may be a historian who has specialized in a field other than the one about which he has written the book you are holding. If so, better skip it and look for someone really steeped in the topic that interests you, a historian who is professional enough to be objective.

I have discussed this problem of anti-Catholic history, especially medieval history, because it so pervasive an issue. It also surfaces in educational videos used by colleges, including mine, to teach history. Here is a description I wrote of a particularly egregious episode in a filmed lecture series by a well-known professor:

> The lecturer is a European historian, obviously not a medievalist, from a university in California. He wants to

reinforce his idea that the Middle Ages were "dark," and makes the asinine observation that when the sun went down it was dark: picture of dark village on the screen. I suppose he thinks the Renaissance had electricity. When he gets to medieval people, he refers repeatedly to the "awkwardness of their minds," being careful not to mention Aquinas, Dante, Abelard, John of Salisbury, or the English physicists. They were so awkward that they built buildings that fell down (painting of a building — actually dating from a later period — that has clearly fallen down). Just when the medievalist is muttering, "What about the cathedrals!" and looking for a brick to heave through the TV, the lecturer admits that the cathedrals existed, that their foundations went down the depth of a subway station and soared hundreds of feet, etc. Then he asks: How, if their minds were so awkward, could they have produced such beauty? Answer: to compensate for the awkwardness of their minds. Question: Would you say there is anything awkward about *his* mind?

If I sound bitter, it is because I know of so much material like this and meet so many people who are amazed when I tell them that the Crusades, for example, were not crimes against humanity. The Middle Ages are probably the period about which the worst books have been written, so it is important to be very careful in choosing your reading if you want to learn the truth. Better to borrow some older works from the library, until you are somewhat familiar with the subject, than to waste money on newer books by unknown authors.

An easy way of finding the names of reliable books is to consult the bibliographies of Catholic historians you know you can trust. Warren Carroll, for example, includes detailed bibliographies in each volume of his *History of Christendom* series, often with comments that indicate how far a certain source can be trusted, and where it is worth consulting. This is invaluable information for anyone wishing to read about specific subjects or start a history book collection.

Once you are sufficiently familiar with Catholic history to want to pursue a special interest and have already utilized the bibliographic references in Catholic history books, it may be time to consult one or more scholars in your chosen field. Historians are usually willing to answer specific inquiries from interested students; indeed, they are often really glad to find someone interested in their area of expertise, in our unhistorically minded age. The Internet has facilitated such scholarly exchanges, and you can often find the website or e-mail address of a historian whose works interest you.

Be forewarned: Once you investigate this deeply into your subject, it may be too late to turn back. History can be positively *addictive*.

ACKNOWLEDGMENTS

This book is based on an ongoing series of articles I have been writing for *The Latin Mass* magazine; I wish to thank Father James McLucas, editor of *The Latin Mass*, for his kind permission to use the material that appears here in book form. I am also very grateful to Thomas Craughwell for encouraging me to take the scary step of writing a book. Without his advice I might never have done it. Finally, I wish to thank Mike Dubruiel and George Foster, my editors at Our Sunday Visitor Publishing, for their encouragement and invaluable suggestions for improving the manuscript.

ABOUT THE AUTHOR

Diane Moczar is adjunct professor of history at Northern Virginia Community College. Dr. Moczar's articles and reviews have appeared in numerous publications, including *Smithsonian*, *San Francisco Chronicle*, *National Review*, and *The Latin Mass*.

A recipient of a Fulbright research scholarship, she studied two years in Paris. She then attended Columbia University, where she received a master's degree in medieval history and also did coursework at the Russian Institute (known today as the Harriman Institute). She completed her doctoral studies at The Catholic University of America and George Mason University.

OSV's Encyclopedia of Catholic History, Revised

Time – and the Church – march on

Still the most comprehensive single-volume compendium on the Church's past – from Pentecost morning to today.

Each entry in this critically-acclaimed and best-selling reference work – first published in 1995 – has been examined for improvement and updating. More than 200 items have been added.

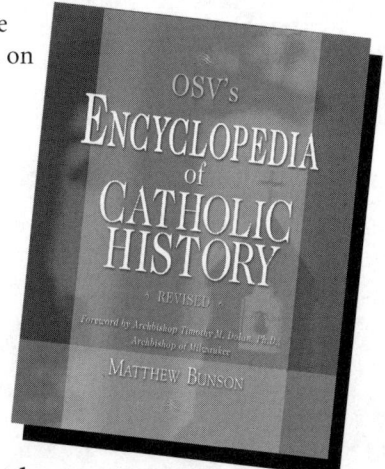

OSV's Encyclopedia of Catholic History, Revised
By Matthew Bunson
1-59276-026-0 (**ID# T77**), hardcover

Available at bookstores. Or, call **1-800-348-2440, ext. 3**. Order online at www.osv.com.

OurSundayVisitor

200 Noll Plaza
Huntington, IN 46750
For a free catalog, call 1-800-348-2440

Availability of books subject to change without notice.

A63BBBBP

Our Sunday Visitor ...
Your Source for Discovering the Riches of the Catholic Faith

Our Sunday Visitor has an extensive line of materials for young children, teens, and adults. Our books, Bibles, pamphlets, CD-ROMs, audios, and videos are available in bookstores worldwide.

To receive a FREE full-line catalog or for more information, call **Our Sunday Visitor** at **1-800-348-2440, ext. 3**. Or write **Our Sunday Visitor** / 200 Noll Plaza / Huntington, IN 46750.

Please send me ___ A catalog
Please send me materials on:
___ Apologetics and catechetics
___ Prayer books
___ The family
___ Reference works
___ Heritage and the saints
___ The parish

Name _____
Address _____ Apt._____
City _____ State _____ Zip_____
Telephone ( ) _____

A63BBBBP

Please send a friend ___ A catalog
Please send a friend materials on:
___ Apologetics and catechetics
___ Prayer books
___ The family
___ Reference works
___ Heritage and the saints
___ The parish

Name _____
Address _____ Apt._____
City _____ State _____ Zip_____
Telephone ( ) _____

A63BBBBP

OurSundayVisitor

200 Noll Plaza, Huntington, IN 46750
Toll free: **1-800-348-2440**
Website: www.osv.com